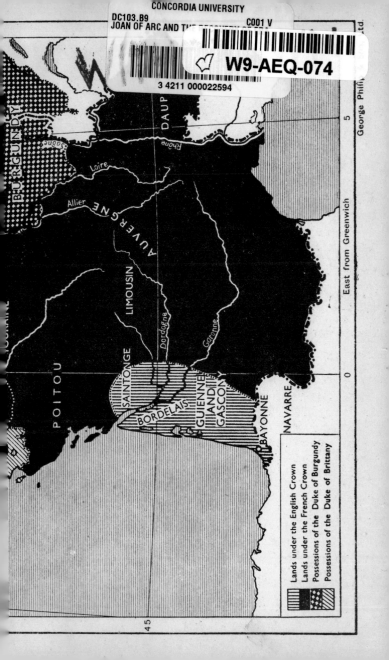

George Philip... ...td.

BURGUNDY

Saône

DAUP

Rhône

Loire

Allier

AUVERGNE

LORRAINE

POITOU

LIMOUSIN

Dordogne

Garonne

SAINTONGE

BORDELAIS

GUIENNE
AND
GASCONY

BAYONNE

NAVARRE

East from Greenwich

5

0

45

Lands under the English Crown
Lands under the French Crown
Possessions of the Duke of Burgundy
Possessions of the Duke of Brittany

JOAN OF ARC

and the

Recovery of France

is one of the volumes
in the
TEACH YOURSELF HISTORY
LIBRARY

Edited by A. L. ROWSE

Teach Yourself History

THE STATUE OF JOAN OF ARC WHICH STANDS BEFORE
THE CATHEDRAL AT RHEIMS

JOAN OF ARC
and the
Recovery of France

by
ALICE BUCHAN

Buchan

Published by
HODDER & STOUGHTON LIMITED
for THE ENGLISH UNIVERSITIES PRESS
AT SAINT PAUL'S HOUSE
IN THE CITY OF LONDON

FIRST PRINTED . JANUARY 1948

PRINTED IN GREAT BRITAIN FOR THE ENGLISH UNIVERSITIES PRESS, LTD.,
LONDON, BY HAZELL, WATSON AND VINEY, LTD., LONDON AND AYLESBURY

A General Introduction to the Series

THIS series has been undertaken in the conviction that there can be no subject of study more important than history. Great as have been the conquests of natural science in our time —such that many think of ours as a scientific age *par excellence*—it is even more urgent and necessary that advances should be made in the social sciences, if we are to gain control of the forces of nature loosed upon us. The bed out of which all the social sciences spring is history; there they find, in greater or lesser degree, subject-matter and material, verification or contradiction.

There is no end to what we can learn from history, if only we would, for it is coterminous with life. Its special field is the life of man in society, and at every point we can learn vicariously from the experience of others before us in history.

To take one point only—the understanding of politics: how can we hope to understand the world of affairs around us if we do not know how it came to be what it is? How to understand Germany, or Soviet Russia, or the United States —or ourselves, without knowing something of their history?

There is no subject that is more useful, or indeed indispensable.

Some evidence of the growing awareness of this may be seen in the immense increase in the interest of the reading public in history, and the much larger place the subject has come to take in education in our time.

This series has been planned to meet the needs and demands of a very wide public and of education—they are indeed the same. I am convinced that the most congenial, as well as the most concrete and practical, approach to history is the biographical, through the lives of the great men whose actions have been so much part of history, and whose careers in turn have been so moulded and formed by events.

The key-idea of this series, and what distinguishes it from any other that has appeared, is the intention by way of a biography of a great man to open up a significant historical theme; for example, Cromwell and the Puritan Revolution, or Lenin and the Russian Revolution.

My hope is, in the end, as the series fills out and completes itself, by a sufficient number of biographies to cover whole periods and subjects in that way. To give you the history of the United States, for example, or the British Empire or France, *via* a number of biographies of their leading historical figures.

That should be something new, as well as convenient and practical, in education.

GENERAL INTRODUCTION

I need hardly say that I am a strong believer in people with good academic standards writing once more for the general reading public, and of the public being given the best that the universities can provide. From this point of view this series is intended to bring the university into the homes of the people.

A. L. Rowse.

All Souls College,
    Oxford.

Contents

To weigh carefully every pertinent fact
is not an occupation which need blind
us to imponderable values.

G. G. COULTON.

Chapter One

The English Occupation of France

TO understand Joan of Arc it is necessary to set her in the frame of the time in which she was born, and turn from the equestrian statues and the dusty laurels, to the soil that bred her and the age that condemned her. It was an age fully as restless and contradictory as our own. If it repudiated Joan, the saviour of her country, for all the wrong reasons, we, in our own enlightened century, are no strangers to like repudiations.

The cautious process of canonization could do no more to make a saint of Joan than the flames that charred her body on that day in May 1431. Just as in life she had refused to behave in an orthodox manner befitting her sex and station, so in death her strong personality, surviving for us in contemporary records, has defied four centuries of man's alternate sentimentalizing and depreciating of her. Her trial for heresy and presumption, and the rehabilitation of her good name twenty-five years later, are the least important things about Joan, who only cared for the trampled soil of her country, which for generations had been overrun by the English invader. The France she knew was leaderless, divided by inherited feuds and racked by misrule. It was her great task to hearten by example the weak yet aspiring spirit of French nationalism.

A backward glance at the circumstances of the people of France and the disputatious oligarchy who, according to one historian of our day, 'lived in a kind of feudal honeymoon, learning nothing, forgetting nothing and foreseeing nothing,' will help us to understand the conditions prevailing in France at the opening of the fifteenth century.

When on Christmas Day, 1066, William Duke of Normandy assumed the crown of England, and the foundations of an Anglo-French empire were laid, there began the infiltration of speech and outlook and the racial assimilation that were to knit England and France closely, though not always in harmony, for the next four centuries. At first it was a fairly 'peaceful permeation.' The similarities of taste and thought, as well as the temperamental differences between the English and the French, provide a picture of alternate attraction and repulsion. The marriage in 1152 of the Conqueror's great-grandson Henry II with Eleanore of Aquitaine dowered England with that great Duchy and extended the Anglo-French empire over the whole of Western France, an empire too diverse and unwieldy for successful administration from England, comprising as it did the heady Gascons, the foreigners of Bayonne and Bigorre, the people of the sea-bordered Bordelais, and the tough feudal baronage of Périgueux and the Limousin.

Henry II, the son of Geoffrey of Anjou, who was called Plantagenet because he wore the yellow broom flower, the *Plantagenista*, as his emblem, was a Frenchman at heart. His far-spread domains included not only Normandy, Maine and Anjou, but his wife's dowry lands of Guienne and Gascony, a racial mixture that needed exceptional gifts of statesmanship to control. He rose to the demand made on him, with a system of centralized government directed from Westminster, and contrived to keep his huge realm in subjection without violence in his lifetime. But by the Treaty of Paris in 1259, in the reign of his grandson Henry III, the English Crown voluntarily renounced certain territorial rights in France and agreed to hold its depleted French empire in homage to the King of France, a compromise that was an attempt to settle the perpetual rivalry between the two countries, which expressed itself in minor but bitter outbreaks of antagonism, the outcome of a growing spirit of nationalism on both sides.

Henry III was as much an Englishman as his grandfather had been a Frenchman, and under him the elaborate system of administration used by Henry II for the governing of his Anglo-French territories shrank and became insular in its application. For England and France were drawing apart, in spite of the fact that the feudal baronage of both countries was closely interrelated, since Duke William's followers had preferred to settle in England, building themselves fortified manors on the French plan, and taking to themselves wives from among the islanders. French was, and would be for generations to come, the language of chivalry and romantic love, and many young Englishmen, feeling themselves cramped at home, preferred to offer their services to influential French nobles and receive from them a military or courtly training. But all the urbanity of French civilization and culture, not stiffened by loyalty to a national ideal, was vulnerable before the invincible English assumption that one Englishman was rather more than a match for three Frenchmen.

One cause of the cleavage was the growing independence of spirit among Englishmen after Edward I perceived that the middle classes must be given status and encouragement if they were amicably to finance the Crown, and had called the first Parliament into consultation; trying, 'by means of an appeal to the lesser folk, to set his authority on a broader basis and get the better of his natural enemies—the great barons and bishops.'[1]

The fabric of Anglo-French friendship was growing threadbare. To reaffirm the interdependence of the two thrones, Edward I married his young son, Edward, to Philip IV's

[1] *France and England in the Middle Ages and Now*, T. F. Tout.

little daughter Isabelle, a marriage that had disastrous results for France, for when Edward II, the child of the marriage, succeeded, the French throne was at the same time threatened with vacancy. Because of his mother Isabelle, Edward III was the next heir, if it had not been for the existence of the Salic law, hurriedly invented by the French, which disallowed inheritance through a woman. The Salic law was a legal convenience, and Edward brushed it aside. On the distaff side he was nearer the French throne than the Valois next-of-kin, who was of a cadet branch, but there were other pretexts and provocations for the Hundred Years War between the two countries that dragged through five English and five French reigns.

The position in France of the English King was, at best, an uncomfortable one, for while he held the dukedoms of Guienne and Gascony he was forced to act counter to, and resist the interference of, his overlord, the King of France, a course of action he would strongly have resented on the part of one of his own feudal barons. It was clearly untenable to hold the position of subject and ruler simultaneously, and most unpalatable to the Plantagenets, inheritors of the restless, despotic temper of the line of Anjou.

Edward III's hand was to a certain extent forced. On his back were the Scots, fermented by propaganda from France, an expensive liability that went with the English crown. The

English territorial interests in western France were shrinking, but on the east the people of Flanders were ready to enter into an alliance with England to protect themselves and their trade. The staple of English commerce had long been the wool trade with Flanders, where fleeces from sheep bred and pastured on Cotswold uplands were spun on Flemish looms into the finest cloth in Europe. An alliance between England and Flanders was thus mutually profitable, and a source of resentment to the French King, who saw Flemish merchants, his own sworn vassals, paying out good money for English wool to be resold to England in the form of cloth. But any attempt on his part to interfere would be countered by an embargo by England on the export of wool, which meant starvation for the cloth-workers of Ghent. Hating their titular overlord, Louis de Nevers, and their pro-French aristocracy, the people of Flanders sent strong encouragement to Edward to grasp his French inheritance and declare his claim to the crown of France. If he lacked pretext for aggression, the depredations on English shipping by pirates in the pay of the French King, off the English coast and along the seaboard of the Low Countries, alone would have provided it.

Every schoolboy knows how the highly-trained English force met the feudal levies of the French King at Crécy in northern France on a rainy evening in August 1346; how the deadly hail of English arrows stampeded the French cavalry, while darkness gathered till no man could tell his brother from his enemy; how in the uproar the French King fled, while many brave Frenchmen fell beside their standards and were trampled in the mud of Picardy, among the lilies of France.

The French army was badly led. Its tactics were out of date. In earlier days, knights, on heavily-encumbered mounts, had formed themselves into close ranks, and charged with couched lances. Against the mobile infantry and the crossbowmen of Edward III's army such clumsy tactics invited destruction. Crécy was to be the first of many victories for the infantry of England.

The names of Crécy and Poitiers sound in our ears after the lapse of centuries like the faint call of bugles carried by the wind across a great distance. No one can hear without pride of the Black Prince, the young son of Edward III, after the battle of Poitiers, receiving in his tent the captured King of France with cordial and courteous words of equal knightly fellowship.

The Hundred Years War was not so much a war as a series of defensive pauses punctuated by bouts of fighting. '. . . It was war of a limited and old-fashioned sort. The French and English knights fought in all courtesy and with a nice regard to the rules of the ring.' This fellowship of honour which bound all knights as one shines with a bright gleam like new metal. On one aspect medieval warfare was a sordid commercial affair; on the other it soared into poetry. No matter that Edward III's claim to the French throne was shaky, that his Flemish allies were dubiously loyal; in spite of it there could emerge from this clash of ambitious natures and the brigandage of sullen mercenaries something indestructible; chivalry in a word.

The Treaty of Brétigny in 1360 ended the first phase of the Hundred Years War. Domestic problems at home, one of which was shortage of money with which to wage war, made Edward decide temporarily to relinquish his claim to the French throne, but to insist, in exchange, on titular sovereignty within the domains that were his by inheritance—Aquitaine in the south, and in the north Ponthieu (his wife's property), and the town of Calais, which had been part of the marriage portion of his grandmother, Eleanore of Castile.

Further, the French were to stop assisting the Scots in their struggle for separate dominion. The Treaty of Brétigny divided and crippled France, and did little good for England beyond the establishing of a strong strategic base for trade and invasion, at Calais.

In the lull that follows the Treaty of Brétigny and the accession of Charles V to the French throne, let us look at conditions in France. Till the end of the thirteenth century conditions for the poorer people were unspeakably bad. In the country the peasants were obliged to pay heavy dues in kind to the local *seigneur* or *gentilhomme* from the starved and meagre ground they had cultivated with their bare hands and a few blunt wooden tools. The *seigneur* might at his pleasure gallop his hounds over the peasant's poor acres, confiscate his corn and vines, indulge himself in robbery, rape, violence, and do so unchecked. In his little world he was supreme, yet in most cases this petty *gentilhomme* could neither read nor write. He lived in a fortified manor house that had a staircase and windows, but his manners were not much better than those of the peasantry who shared a one-roomed hovel with the beasts of the field.

Though he was a little king in his own little kingdom, he in his turn was the vassal of some lord or knight who could command his services in time of war. In between wars he endured a monotonous existence on his estates, varied only by persecution of those humbler and more helpless than himself, while the peasant dragged out a wretched existence in perpetual terror of his master's justice.

The living conditions of the peasant were the lowest possible; his cottage was cramped, unventilated, and damp in winter. A fire kindled on a stone in the middle of the floor filled it with choking smoke. The only piece of furniture would be a bed to accommodate the whole family. The peasant's daily diet was porridge, black bread, and, if he was lucky, fat bacon. Under this roof, along with his hens and his pig,

9

his family lived without the means of privacy. Worse than the hard conditions of poverty was the hopelessness of their state. They might not migrate to another village nor marry out of the district. The crowding together of families in this way resulted in incest with its tragic consequences of disease and lunacy, but a rise in the birth-rate was more or less counter-balanced by mortality from epidemics, or famine when the crops failed.

Thus the feudal system, which had evolved naturally from the need of the unprotected for protection, had changed its character, and the balance of give and take between the villein and his protector was no longer maintained: the relationship became one of oppression on the one hand and slavishness on the other.

Toward the middle of the fourteenth century conditions began very gradually to improve. Money began to be more plentiful, and if a peasant could get to the market in a nearby town and sell his produce there, he might come home with a tidy sum. After a time the village elders would put their takings together and make up a sum large enough to purchase a *carte de franchise*. The *seigneur*, who was always in need of money, sold them, by this means, the right to become freemen, which meant that they could leave his domain and marry outside it, if they desired, without his sanction. This did not mean that all the villeins became freemen, or that the *seigneur* always kept his pledged word. Nor were living conditions thereby much improved. But it was the beginning of better things.

The Hundred Years War loosed a new terror on the peasantry. The men rode away from the villages in their lord's train, glad, perhaps, of a respite from the monotony of their existence. The place was left to women and old men with no effective weapons for defence.

It made little difference which way the tide of battle went. At the first lull in hostilities the country would be flooded with *brigandines*, so-called from the short coats of mail they wore, intent on plunder. There being no standing army in France at that time, the army of the Crown was made up of companies of mercenaries, or professional fighting men, recruited by a leader who might be a *gentilhomme*, or the younger son of a noble family. The leader was expected to make himself personally responsible for the maintenance of his men, but too often they never saw any payment, and were obliged to fall back on plunder in order to live, as there was no organization for feeding and equipping the troops.

The mercenary soldier considered himself entitled to take what he could by force. War was a business; he signed on for a stated period, indifferent to the cause at issue, determined to make what he could out of it.

Nor were all soldiers of fortune of low birth. The feudal leaders were not much more scrupulous than their men, from the great nobles who were vassals of the Crown, to the country squireens who were vassals of the local baron. It was a common practice for bands of these fire-brands to surround a town and demand ransom; if bribes were not immediately offered they would pillage the houses and burn what was not movable, before seeking plunder elsewhere. Women and children made for the woods at their approach. After Poitiers the systematic havoc wreaked by these freebooting bands was appalling.

A contemporary has described the later years of the war in words applicable to the whole period: '. . . the spoil and ravage is so general, that our unhappy peasants, for all their sweat and unceasing labour are scarcely left—I will not say with wheaten bread—but even with rye-bread wherewith to drag out their wretched existence. What can I say of their clothing when their persecutors, even in mid-winter, will rob them of the very sackcloth they ordinarily wear, unless it be too old and ragged ?'[1]

A rising in Paris of the townspeople in 1307, headed by the burgesses, had shown the mounting temper of the people at the selfish tyranny of their feudal lords. An attempt was made to force the Dauphin to set his hand to a Charter of Liberties—a French parallel to Magna Charta. But with the English at their gates, the moment was ill-chosen; and the seed of revolt, once sown,

[1] Nicolas de Clemanges, Archdeacon of Bayeux.

sprang into intimidating life in the rank soil of corruption. The peasant might be slow and illiterate, but he had a long memory. The *Jacques*, as the villeins were called—*Jacques Bonhomme* being the popular catchword for the ordinary man, as John Bull is in our country— rose in long-fermented fury. The barons, angry and afraid, summoned their mercenaries. 'The *Jacquerie*, which was characterized, as every rising of the desperate poor is apt to be, by great ferocity, was put down with ease, but the country was no stronger for that bitter victory, nor for the terrible social chasm which it left behind it.'

Charles V, whose father had been taken prisoner by the English at Poitiers, came to the throne in 1364. He ruled arbitrarily, imposing taxes with a heavy hand, yet lived to be called the Wise, perhaps because his reign revived the stricken prestige of French military power, under a great leader, Bertrand du Guesclin. This wise Breton soldier was able to instil some respect for discipline into the insubordinate professional soldiery; as Constable of France he became a figure of legend.

Edward, the Black Prince, had set up his court at Bordeaux in the centre of his great principality of Aquitaine. He maintained order with an iron hand, but not always with his rival's discretion. His last years were warped by sickness and failure. Once the brightest ornament of chivalry, in his decline the sick lion made his name unhappily memorable by acts of cruelty and intolerance.

13

A flare of his old war-loving spirit impelled him across the Pyrénées to take sides in a tussle for the crown of Spain between Pedro of Castile and his half-brother Henry. The rigours of that campaign halved the fighting strength of his mercenary army, who crawled home sick, disgruntled and clamorous for pay.

The moment was ripe and Du Guesclin struck blow after lightning blow till by 1374 all of Poitou and much of Guienne and Gascony were back in the hands of the French. Pedro of Castile, who was as mean as infamous, refused to recognize obligation to his partisans. The taxes levied by the Black Prince on the Duchy of Aquitaine to pay for the Spanish expedition moved the proud, always resentful, Gascons to appeal to the French King. It was bitter for Edward to receive a summons from Paris to attend the judgment of his peers, as if he were himself no better than a vassal of the Crown of France. His scornful answer contained an ineffectual threat and in 1371 he limped back to England to die. Du Guesclin had brilliantly 'systematized that plan of campaign which successfully avoided pitched battles and wore down the victors by a desultory war of sieges and skirmishes.'

'*Estoc d'honneur et arbre de vaillance*,' the poet Eustache Deschamps called him:

'*Coeur de lion, esprins d'hardement,*
La fleur des preux et la gloire de France. . . .'

14

The great tree, the lion heart, the white flower of courtesy, these were Bertrand du Guesclin. When he fell, wounded to death, men could scarcely believe he would not rise and fight again. Charles did not long survive the death of his great Constable. He had during his reign given his people back some of their birthright, and a measure of prosperity. He had been sickly from birth; the wonder is not that he died young, but that his failing body survived so long.

The Black Prince was now dead, and his father, the old King Edward III of England, did not long outlive him. The Black Prince's ten-year-old son had been born in France, and was known, from the name of his birthplace, as Richard of Bordeaux. This boy was from the first subjected to the contemptuous and heavy-handed regency of his father's three brothers. But he was not a prince of putty, as was his contemporary on the throne of France, Charles the Wise's eleven-year-old son, Charles VI. There is a certain parallel in their situations, but none in the character of the two boys. Charles VI of France was afflicted with a disease of the brain which threw him from time to time into a deep melancholy, and in this state he was not able to endure sudden noises or movement, and would strike about him with his sword, till his attendants disarmed him.

The relapse of France into civil war that took place after the death of Charles V was due to a spirit of 'fierce faction' engendered by the

King's three paternal uncles, the royal Dukes of Anjou, Berry and Burgundy, and his maternal uncle the Duke of Bourbon, all irreconcilably ambitious and quarrelsome. The long minority of the young King and the tragedy of his growing insanity gave them full scope to indulge their jealous rivalry. The very name of Burgundy is like a mutter of thunder. For many years to come the greed and power of the Burgundian house were to overcast the skies of France.

In England, Richard of Bordeaux had for a brief time, after coming of age, shaken off the yoke of inauspicious stars. Believing that in peace with France lay the only salvation of his own country, he took, as his second wife, the King of France's little daughter, Isabelle of Valois. The truce which he set his hand to on this occasion was intended to last for thirty years. King Richard was not destined himself to outlive it and, like the Treaty of Brétigny, it was soon to be dishonoured, and not worth the parchment it was inscribed on.

A calculated act of revenge, the banishment of his first cousin, Henry of Lancaster, and the confiscation of the Lancastrian estates and their revenues, brought about King Richard's downfall.

He was visiting Ireland in 1399 when Lancaster returned secretly and landed in Yorkshire. The country rose to him. Hurrying back from Ireland to meet his usurping cousin, Richard found very few to support him, for his growing monomania

for revenge on the men who had soured his youth
had made him increasingly unpopular with his
nobility, just as the extravagance and craving for
personal power which had replaced his youthful
fastidious love of peace and order had alienated
him from his people. Before two months were out,
Richard was a prisoner and Henry of Lancaster
led the country and was crowned at Westminster
as Henry IV.

To the French princes it offered fresh opportunity for partisanship and division. The King's
younger brother, Louis, Duke of Orléans, flung
himself with zeal into the cause of the deposed
Richard, of whose fate nothing was known, though
dark things were suspected. The century in
France was ending in anarchy, famine and
depravity, and Louis of Orléans was typical of
those in the ascendancy who exalted licence and
misrule above order and justice. During this
comparative lull of preoccupation with internal
affairs on the part of England, under a strong rule
France might have come to terms with the English
Crown. Instead of which the French princes
made each the terms that suited their individual
ambitions, and baited the enemy with airy and
ambiguous promises of the restoration of Aquitaine
and the reconquest of Normandy.

In 1404 John the Fearless succeeded to his
father's Dukedom of Burgundy and, with a
sharper eye to the main chance, made overtures
of friendship to Richard's successor. There was

a deep and bitter rivalry between himself and his cousin of Orléans, who by that time had begun to be regarded with alarm by the people of Paris on account of the openness of his liaison with the Queen (a German princess, Isabelle of Bavaria). When he was set upon one evening as he was returning alone from the Queen's apartments and hacked in pieces, John of Burgundy was loudest of all in the outcry against his cousin's murderer, but he found it prudent to retire to his estates for a time. There could be no shadow of doubt about who had instigated the murder.

The blood of Louis d'Orléans crying from the stones of the alley where he fell, with fifty wounds in his body, called for revenge. His young son, the new Duke of Orléans, had for father-in-law a Gascon nobleman called Bernard, Count of Armagnac. The name of Armagnac is significant, for it is one that constantly recurs through the years that follow. It became the name of the party which vowed to avenge Orléans and bring about the downfall of Burgundy. It was the side upon which Joan of Arc was to range herself in the name of God and His Saints.

Here was a clear issue and it split the country— in the west and south the Armagnacs could count on the Normans, Bretons and Gascons, in the north and east Burgundy commanded the allegiance of the men of Picardy, Flanders and Lorraine. Of the two factions Burgundy was the more popular with the people of Paris, for the

Armagnacs were identified in their minds with the licentiousness of the Court, and the old oppressive feudal order.

The intermittent civil war of the following years ended in a partial patched-up reconciliation, brought about by the desperate state of the country, its empty exchequer, the apathy of its cowed and hungry peasantry and the depredations of the feudal mercenaries. Appeals to England from both parties from time to time lured over expeditionary forces which did nothing to resolve the issue.

After wearing his uneasy crown for thirteen years Henry of Lancaster died while praying for his soul in Westminster Abbey, and was succeeded by his young son Henry, with whom a new menace to France was born.

There now sat upon the throne of England a King strangely compounded of ruthlessness and piety. He had been, while Prince of Wales, addicted to acts of rowdyism in taverns, common to high-spirited young men whose fathers keep them in a state of repression. But from his accession all that was changed. Forgotten all in an hour were the likeable follies of his youth. From the first he made it clear that he would tolerate no aspersions upon the validity of his claim to the English throne, and told his Ministers that God had called him to unite once again the lilies of France with the leopards of England. He was no fanatic, but a disciplined, forcible personality;

spare in appearance, austere in outlook, he was unamenable to flattery, indifferent to easy living, not to be dazzled by rich promises, or intimidated by threats. Above all, he was no lover of war for its own sake. He was reviving Edward III's claim, but with a difference. He dreamed of a united Christendom, and believed it to be in his power to bring it about. In his stern vision of an orderly and united Europe, Henry ignored the dubiousness of his own claim to the English throne. The victory of Agincourt, that halved at a blow the chivalry of France, established beyond doubt Henry's popularity with his own people. It has been proved again and again (and in our own times) that nothing demoralizes a people's judgment like a successful war. The Treaty of Brétigny, which was worthless since neither side respected it, was declared void. Once more the English shipyards hummed, and the bowyers tipped their ash wands with the grey goose's feather.

On Sunday the 11th of August 1415, that great vessel, the *Trinity*, foremost of the English fleet, caught the first puff of the fair wind that set her sails for France. Many men of that expeditionary force fell below the walls of the port of Harfleur, and more perished of a virulent dysentery, contracted in the fever-ridden marsh country round about the town, in which the English armies lay at night. It was an August of exceptional heat. A diet of fruit and shellfish aggravated the plague. The English army, disease-stricken and impoverished in numbers, can hardly have been a sight to gladden their leader's eyes, when after the successful subjugation of Harfleur he gave the order to march.

A hundred-odd miles lay between them and the English-occupied port of Calais, where he hoped to entrench his force till England could send reinforcements. Along the coastline of northern France, expectant every moment of an ambush, the English made slow headway. Looting was unconditionally forbidden and the King had ordained the death penalty for violence to women and priests. This was not like the freebooters of the Black Prince; soberly and in silence the men plodded after their leaders.

In the meantime, while Burgundy stayed his hand, the French army, led by the supporters of the Orléanist cause and the house of Valois, was moving to intercept the forces of the English King. Hearing of this, Henry was obliged to look for a place favourable for engagement, since an engagement was to be forced upon him. He made a huge detour in order to cross the river Somme, and on Thursday, 24th of October, brought his dog-weary men to a halt in an undulating country of woods and cornfields nearby the little hamlet of Agincourt.

There was no elation in the English ranks. The French camp flared all night with torches and rang with shouting and laughter; in the opposite camp all was silence and darkness. Priests moved noiselessly from tent to tent hearing the confessions in whispers.

All that night it rained. As soon as the morning light came, the English archers made a palisade of six-foot wooden stakes, behind which to take up their position. Everyone, including the King and his brothers, fought on foot.

The French outnumbered the English by three to one, but their army was a disorderly affair, lacking leadership. It was drawn up on the morning of St. Crispin's Day, October 25th, in three blocks of cavalry, packed closely one behind the other. Because the front rank was the position of honour, there was gathered the chivalry of France.

The *gens d'armes* who had come from their *manoires* to fight disputed pride of place with the cross-bowmen and stationed themselves in the forefront, where they were so pressed for space they could not effectively handle their pikes. All but these were mounted. All were weightily armed, where the Englishmen wore only leather doublets with light helmets of steel.

From the front the French must have seemed a redoubtable force, with banners flying and horses champing; they had chosen, too, the more advantageous position on a slight rise of ground.

It was near ten in the morning before both sides were marshalled within striking distance. When the English cheer rang blithely out, as it has rung down the centuries ever since, '*Haro! Haro! St. George for Merry England!*'—the French cavalry moved forward.

For a cavalry charge to be effective it must have the impetus of distance. Archers, on the other hand, are deadly at short range. The French horsemen, weighted with their armour, had difficulty in advancing across the soft ground which quickly turned to a morass under their horses' feet. As those who were in front fell, under the steady and terrible rain of English arrows, those behind were pushed forward by the great weight of numbers, and, stumbling, floundered in the deep mud. The size of the French side was its undoing. There was no courage wanting; the French princes, the Dukes of Orléans, Bourbon and Alençon, the Counts of Nevers, Vaudemont, and Fauquemberg, to mention a very few, fought bravely, but there was no coherence. They were not, and had never been, of one mind. They could not control their stampeding mounts or the undisciplined mass of their feudal levies— that 'rabble of disorderly footmen that the aristocrats regarded with contempt and rode down without scruple. . . .'

At the crucial moment, a moment of which they had been warned and for which they were ready, the English archers abandoned their bows and hacked their way among the French with short maces and billhooks, weapons that were deadly in effect in the packed, struggling mass.

For two or three hours the fighting raged, until the dead were heaped high. Buried and half-suffocated in one of these mounds was the young Duke of Orléans, the titular leader of the Orléanist or Armagnac party, whom the English King made his prisoner.

When Gascon and Breton reinforcements came up they perceived their leaders' standards to be in English hands, and retired without giving battle. When, finally, the 'Cease fighting' order was sounded the sun was declining and a light rain had begun to fall. In the churned mud lay thousands of the flower of France; the English losses were not much above one hundred. It was a magnificent piece of bluff on the part of Henry V and could not have succeeded had not the French generals been divided in aim. The French never again during Henry's lifetime met the English in open battle.

Henry returned to England to celebrate, among scenes of frantic rejoicing, the victory of Agincourt. He received overtures from the French princes, and wary ambassadors passed to and fro across the Channel. From Germany the Emperor expressed his desire for an alliance between England, France and Germany that would exclude and limit the power of the House of Burgundy. The project of a marriage between the English King and Princess Catherine of France was discussed. Henry, the cool strategist, knew very well that eventually the sword alone would decide the issue, but while a waiting game suited his purposes he could play it with the best. It would take time to recruit and equip another army capable of the huge task of beating France to her knees, and a pause now would give the French a sense of helpless insecurity, not knowing where next the blow might fall.

When for the second time his flagship, the *Trinity*, took the sea it was for Normandy. Again the advantage fell to the English. Caen, with its stately abbeys, Falaise, the birthplace of the Conqueror, Bayeux and others, were in English hands by the spring of 1418. Normandy was a strategic gain; from there it would be possible for the English to send harrying expeditions into the Armagnac strongholds in Anjou and Maine. But the sullen, independent Normans, though conquered, were by no means amenable to English rule; it was clear that if the English King intended to prosecute the war elsewhere he would have to leave a strong army of occupation to protect his interests in Normandy.

He now turned his attention to Rouen, the second city of France, and after a long, desperate and bitter siege, lasting through the winter and past the Christmas of 1418, the proud city opened its gates to him. This slow starvation of civilians and the ruthless punishing of resistant towns left a great impression on contemporary historians. According to one, the townspeople after six months of siege were reduced to eating 'cattis,

hors, houndis, rattis, myse. . . .' When King
Henry entered the city after its capitulation it is
recorded that he rode, looking neither to right
nor left, and prayed alone far into the night;
no doubt pleading to God the tortuous self-
justification that obsessed him.

By this time (1419), characters who are later to
play their parts in the drama of Joan of Arc begin
to emerge from the shadowy, turbulent throng.
The two elder sons of the mad King Charles VI
of France had died; their brother Charles thus
became Dauphin.

Charles, whom we are to see later as a weak and
dilatory King, was a pliable boy controlled by the
Armagnac faction. Behind the Dauphin stands
his mother, Queen Isabelle. We have no reliable
portrait of her and can only judge her character
by her actions. Urged by the Armagnacs, the
Dauphin Charles flung off her domination. That
it was a rough, contemptuous domination can be
guessed from the fact that she said openly, not
caring who overheard, that he was a bastard and
not the rightful heir at all. Charles had a nasty
crooked temper of his own, to match his awkward,
knock-kneed frame. His banishment of her sent
the Queen-mother to the arms of her old lover,
the Duke of Burgundy, and with her the power of
attorney she held for the Crown, as self-appointed
regent for the mad King.

Bernard of Armagnac was even more hated
and feared than John of Burgundy, for his Gascon

soldiery were cruel and ruthless beyond all bounds. When, in May 1418, the Burgundians surprised the Armagnacs who were lodged in Paris, the people, driven to desperation, burst out of their houses and thronged the streets, crying *'Death to the Gascon!'* and *'Long live Burgundy!'* The Dauphin was hustled away by the Provost of Paris. For a fortnight the city was in an uproar. The leaders of the Armagnac party were flung into prison, but the mob beat down the walls of the Conciergerie and tore them in pieces. Bernard of Armagnac was among the victims. The Queen made a triumphal entry when the worst of the mess had been cleared up, and John of Burgundy shared her triumph.

The Armagnac-Orléanists, henceforward to be called the Dauphinists, were now in the minority. They entrenched themselves at Poitiers to plan vengeance. Burgundy, though in the ascendant, was uneasy about the war with England, for with Rouen in his hands the English King was in an alarmingly strong position. But Henry himself was not over-anxious for more fighting. The garrisons in Normandy were giving him trouble. War was a costly business and his soldiers must be paid if they were not to break loose after plunder. The siege of Rouen had been a lengthy, dispiriting affair. They were a long way from home, and the victorious march into Paris which they had been promised seemed no nearer.

But he was equally determined (and his was

a nature to which compromise made no appeal) to reaffirm the terms of the maligned Treaty of Brétigny, and insist on the restoration of Normandy and Aquitaine as the price of peace. He was prepared to relinquish his claim to the French crown and receive instead the French King's daughter in marriage.

After a formal meeting of King Henry with the Duke of Burgundy at Meulan in the spring of 1419, at which Queen Isabelle was present with her daughter, Princess Catherine, the Dauphinists began to panic. It occurred to them that they had better join issue with Burgundy, before the Queen married off her daughter to the English King and pushed her son (whose legitimacy she allowed it to be known was doubtful) off the throne of France. The more moderate followers of the Dauphin and Burgundy had been trying for some time to bring about that reconciliation, imploring them to sink their mutual dislike in the interest of their country. At last Burgundy reluctantly agreed, and the Dauphin fretfully consented to a meeting which was arranged to take place in the September of 1419 at Montereau, a little walled town that bridged the joining of the rivers Seine and Yonne.

To show good faith, the Dauphin ceded the castle to Burgundy and himself lodged in the town. They were to meet on the bridge over the river. The followers of Burgundy were apprehensive, but the Duke was not nicknamed '*Jean sans Peur*' for nothing. Saying stoutly that one must risk something for the cause of peace, he set out for the fatal rendezvous. As the Duke knelt before his Prince, an Armagnac from behind clove his head open with an axe. *53778*

No one knew who was behind the murder, which was as low and cowardly an act as that by which Louis d'Orléans had met his death at his cousin's hands twelve years before. The Dauphin was hustled away in a state of collapse; all his life he protested innocence of any knowledge that the murder was premeditated. No suspicion of English complicity clung to the affair. Almost the last boast the Duke had been heard to utter was that no man, and certainly no Englishman, was his master.

When the news was brought to the English King he brooded on it with the rapt visionary look that his associates knew well. Through that axe-hole in the Duke of Burgundy's skull he saw the road to Paris open. He had known how to play a waiting game; now his patience was to be rewarded. Isabelle the Queen, with the murdered Duke's son, Philip of Burgundy, the Burgundian Party and the people of Paris, flung their pride away and clamoured for English vengeance for their lost leader. Where before the English King's claims had been regarded as fantastic and exorbitant, he was now invited to name his own terms. It seemed as if the Dauphin's cause was hopeless against such an alliance. The bitter mortification forced on the weak, unamiable Charles was vented by him on his bad advisers. His hour was to come, though by no strength of will or self-denial on his part.

Henry undertook to relinquish his claim to the title of King of France during King Charles VI's lifetime, and to assume the rôle of Regent with absolute power. He agreed to allow his conquests of French terrain to revert to the Crown of France, and to respect and uphold the French Parliament and the Church. The mad King's poor, trembling hand set the imprint of the Royal House of Valois to the soft wax that sealed the agreement. The new peace was sworn at Troyes, and Henry's betrothal and marriage to the Princess Catherine followed immediately after.

Henry only had two more years in which to enjoy this conditional triumph. Two years of honestly trying to restore some measure of prosperity to France, and to reconcile quarrelsome elements at home that had got out of hand during his prolonged absences abroad. He died at the age of thirty-five. A virulent dysentery had taken hold of his system during the long, wet winter sieges, which the rough experimental medicines of the period did nothing to alleviate.

With his dying breath he was heard to exclaim: 'Lord, Thou knowest it was my desire to rebuild the walls of Jerusalem.' The victor of Agincourt carried to the grave his impracticable conception of a united Christendom, which he had preserved through the rigours of the seven years' campaign. He left England a son of mixed Plantagenet and Valois blood, and France incompletely subjected, with Burgundians and Dauphinists like growling curs, insecurely chained. Many of the French mourned a conqueror whom they honoured as having been '*sobre de bouche, véritable en parolles, haut et élevé en courage.*'

To the warring princes of France, Henry's campaigns were but ripples on the dark flood of their inherited blood feud. Most of the country south of the Loire was Dauphinist in sympathy, and still strongly feudal. To the enslaved peasants of that region no rumours had penetrated of the English King who forbade swearing and looting among his soldiers, who walked on foot among his men, dressed simply like any other knight, and shared their vigils and their hardships. Their princes were not of that austere pattern. Yet many were to live to see the standard of their country borne to victory by a young girl, poor, and of peasant stock like themselves, in whose presence blasphemous words parched on the lips that framed them.

But this was in the future still. In August 1422 the ten-year-old daughter of Jacques d'Arc was driving a neighbour's sheep to pasture. The voice of God and His Saints had not yet been heard in Domrémy.

Chapter Two

The Daughter of Jacques d'Arc

CHARLES VI, the mad King of France, died not quite two months after his English son-in-law. Neglected by his attendants, who impudently spent the money which the English King provided for his comfort, he had sunk into a pitiful state of dirt and degradation. The nine-months-old baby cradled at Windsor who had been declared King of England and France (putting aside the claims of the Dauphin Charles which were discredited by the Treaty of Troyes) was heir to a very mixed heredity. With Henry VI, the House of Lancaster was to decline from its short-lived splendour. His was the helplessness of a fastidious spirit born into a world that is too rough for it, and he was unfitted both temperamentally and physically for the struggle of life. Posterity was to make a saint of this weak English King as it did of the strong French peasant girl who was his scourge and enemy.

After Henry V's death his brother Bedford, whom the dead king had named Regent of France, was determined that no effort of his should be spared to make the English King's last journey memorable to the French. An effigy was

made, crowned and robed, and carried on an
open litter. It was to be escorted to Calais, and
on the way to pause in every town in which the
King had set his conquering foot, so that a last
homage might be paid.

Bedford himself accompanied the procession
as far as Rouen; there he wrung the hands of his
old comrades-in-arms, and turned back to take
up his great burden. Ten days later he was chief
and sole mourner at the grave of the mad King
of France. No French nobles attended that
shabby interment, but the people of Paris wept
when they saw the coffin carried through the
streets. They had cherished a legend that could
he but throw off his malady, their good King
Charles would rise and save them from the horror
of civil war and the menace of foreign invasion.
Bedford saw their tears; his own heart can scarcely
have been light. His esquire rode before him
carrying the Sword of State, that descended, it
was said, through the French Kings from
Charlemagne.

His was an unenviable task, and though his
part in hounding Joan of Arc to her death is
what is chiefly remembered of him, it is recorded
that his rule in France was just and equable.

He was in every way a reflection of his elder
brother, imitator of his methods, pledged to continue Henry V's life work along the lines on which
the great Lancastrian had launched it, single-
mindedly bent on carrying out this ungrateful

and arduous task without thought of self. His administration was supple, moderate wherever possible, brutal only when necessary. His manners had the dry reserve that most Englishmen have who are forced by circumstances to live out of England. His innate fair-mindedness made him see both sides' points of view, though it was his misfortune to be frequently misjudged. A lover of the orderly and gentle things of life, of beautiful manuscripts and music, it was his fate to be endlessly and wearily involved in slippery diplomacy and unrewarded attempts to reconcile quarrelsome factions.

The last two years of Henry V's life had seen the taking of several Dauphinist strongholds on the Loire and in northern France; Henry's last great military operation was the siege and capture of the town of Meaux on the Marne, not long before he fell ill of his last fatal illness. In spite of this the inheritance of the little King at Windsor was precarious. The Treaty of Troyes had been solemnly and piously ratified, but it was only a piece of parchment. England now possessed by inheritance the Duchy of Guienne, in the south-west, and by conquest and agreement most of the country north of the Loire—Normandy, Picardy, and Champagne, and all the coast from Calais to Mont St. Michel. Brittany and Flanders ceded doubtful and grudging alliance to the English Crown, and were by no means to be relied upon. The river Loire roughly cuts France in two, horizontally. Most of the country to the south of it (the larger part) was Dauphinist in sympathy, though there were pockets of English occupation.

War with England had now been going on intermittently over a period of about seventy-odd years. The men who had borne arms at Crécy against Edward III had long ago died, and their great-grandsons were growing into manhood. There had been long pauses between the English invasions, but little respite from the consequences of feudal tyranny. The plight of Dauphinist France was wretched enough. It had taken all Henry V's firmness to restrain his men from plundering. In the Dauphin's entourage no one cared how the soldiers occupied themselves when they were not required to fight. Lawlessness is infectious; the peasants, with low moral standards, no education, no future, and no redress, knew only one law, that of the survival of the fittest.

But since the days of Charles the Wise the burgher class had been expanding. These rich tradespeople, who were, of course, only to be found in the towns, were ready to lend out money to finance wars. This growing middle-class fostered the seed of nationalism that was soon to put forth root and branch. Their children would get an education of a very elementary kind; they would learn in time to rise above the hard, narrow conditions of their lives. By the

35

fifteenth century the town-dwellers, having got some measure of freedom, were beginning to show the lively, shrewd, critical, fluent, satirical turn of mind and speech that has been handed down to their descendants of today. A child of this century, François Villon, wrote deathless verse between bouts of drunkenness in a Paris gutter. The voice of Villon, that was the strangled voice of the people of France, spoke from the depths of hunger and poverty with a raucous accent, ready to drop into a beggar's whine. It was coarse, quarrelsome, subversive, vain, and impudent: but it was a living voice.

In the country the peasants moved more slowly. The dead hand of an ancient tyranny lay heavier than ever since the fiasco of the *Jacquerie*, the rising of the poor, made desperate by want and oppression, against their overlords. With a sort of patient fatalism they watched their thrifty fields laid waste, and turned to and dug over the wreckage. Human nature is a sturdy plant and can adapt itself to almost any soil. The legacy of grasping landlords, thieving soldiery, and the high price of bread they accepted, for even in their great-grandfathers' recollection it had been so. It is doubtful if villages and hamlets, lying, as did the village of Domrémy, far from the scenes of the fighting and from the main highways, had more than a hazy idea of who was fighting who, and why.

On the death of the old, mad King, the Dauphin's following had immediately proclaimed him King of France. Though Bedford hurried to reaffirm the clauses of the Treaty of Troyes, he could not shake Frenchmen from their inner conviction that, whatever were the political views they held at the moment, the eldest and only son of the anointed King of France was by divine right the successor to the throne. Had Charles but known it, the English foothold in France was more precarious than it seemed; his own place in the hearts of Frenchmen a warmer one, for his dynasty's sake, than he dreamed of. A bold front would have won over to his side many waverers, but it was not in him to take a bold initiative. He preferred to skulk at one or other of his shadow-courts, bickering with his pages, while the nobles, clergy, and generals of his entourage made plans over his head and ignored him. Not that he cared; he only wanted to be left alone to lead the sort of pampered existence that appealed to him. He was not so much a coward as that the littlenesses of life bulked large to him. He had a terror of catching cold, of sitting in a draught, of getting his feet wet. His portrait shows him dressed in thick padded velvet, furred to the knuckles. Nothing about him, neither his character nor his physical make-up, commanded respect.

Bedford may sometimes have wished himself an adversary worthier of his mettle. He got one—in Joan of Arc. But she being a woman, and, as he believed, a limb of the Fiend, demoniacally inspired, he gave her no credit.

He had his misgivings about his ally Philip of Burgundy. But Henry V's dying command had been 'conciliate Burgundy,' and he concealed his rising sense of exasperation at the futility of words, and called a meeting at Amiens in 1423, that was to seal a new tripartite alliance between England, Burgundy, and Brittany. His only surviving brother, Humfry of Gloucester, was quite without moral scruple, and the only family resemblance between them seems to have been his scholarly interests, which make him remembered as a patron of learning. As a statesman he was without substance, lacking his brother's balance of mind and capable judgment. Restless and unreliable, his presence on the Council at home was a danger to the English interests in France, since the friction between Duke Humfry and his Beaufort uncle, the Cardinal of Winchester, whom the dead king had named as one of the guardians of his son, was a perpetual drag on Bedford's overburdened and preoccupied mind. To curb Humfry and conciliate Philip, took all the Regent's determined tact. In an effort to cement Anglo-Burgundian friendship, he took in marriage Philip's youngest sister, the Lady Anne. We hear of this kindly Duchess when Joan of Arc was imprisoned in Rouen at the mercy of English and Burgundian soldiers.

Anne sent her a dress to replace the man's attire that so offended her judges.

Bedford was well aware that his ally's only thought was to increase his own prestige and power at the expense of whatever side he might be on at the moment. Philip of Burgundy was too bland, too talkative, too ready with phrases. He was a type of the age, a *faux bonhomme*; the lavishness of his establishments, the number of his mistresses, was a matter for wonder to chroniclers of the day. His father's murder had goaded him to a blind fury of revenge, of which England was the instrument, but once his blood had cooled he repudiated the finer shades of obligation.

In 1424 Philip of Burgundy was offered full justification for falling out with England. Briefly, Humfry of Gloucester had contracted a liaison with a runaway Duchess of Brabant, who was, in her own right, heiress of Hainault. Now both Brabant and Hainault were geographically extremely important to Burgundy, linking the duchy with its vassal state of Flanders. The lady was, moreover, Duke Philip's own first cousin, and her marriage to the ruler of Brabant had been a family arrangement, designed to establish a solid block of territory in the north-eastern corner of Europe. Her marriage to Duke Humfry was no marriage at all; her divorce was unratified by Rome. All Bedford's warnings could not prevent his volatile brother from launching an army across the Channel with the intention of helping himself to his mistress's rich provinces. The rupture was prevented from becoming serious; Gloucester having fallen out of love with the Countess and in love with one of her ladies, the marriage was annulled and Burgundy appeased. The rift in the Anglo-Burgundian alliance was shakily patched up again, but the fabric was wearing extremely threadbare.

In his shadow-capital at Bourges, Charles VII of France, sunk in apathy, dawdled away his days. He was not consulted by his generals, and the councils of his ministers more often than not excused his attendance. But being a Valois—it is difficult to accept Queen Isabelle's careless statement of his illegitimacy—he was not wholly without pride. Though he feared and shunned responsibility, he was enough of a prince to feel a fretting discontent at the plight of his country, which broke out occasionally in pointless outbursts of temper, vented against one or other of his entourage. They did not quite laugh aloud in his face, but behind his back the poor figure he cut, with his knock-knees and bony wrists and bulbous nose, was the subject of ill-natured caricature.

All this while in a village on the borders of Lorraine, the child Joan was growing up.

After her death, inevitably, legends clustered like weeds about the scenes of her childhood, and their strangling growth obscures the simple facts. She was born of poor, but not abjectly poor, parents. Jacques d'Arc was a farmer in a very small way. He had married a woman called Isabelle Romée from a neighbouring village, and together they reared up a family of five in stringency and the fear of God.

Jacques seems to have been well respected locally and at different times acted for the local landowner as collector of taxes and tributes, and on behalf of the village in a dispute with the governor of a nearby garrison town. He was a stern father, possibly from a conviction of his own infallibility, and partly from strict Catholic rectitude. On summer evenings when the village worthies gathered about the pump to arbitrate the affairs of the community, they would be silent till Jacques d'Arc had spoken. He was a type which persists to this day in all countries; a man who acts according to simple, unswerving standards, suspicious of change, tenacious of slowly-milled opinions. Such a man as only the country life produces, stiff and hard and narrow —the hardening and stiffening process having been going on in him from early contact with harsh weather and bad farming conditions, the narrowness coming from an intense religious conviction, channelling not wide, but deep.

Of his wife Isabelle even less is known, except that long after Joan's trial and death, though aged and crippled, she appealed for a retrial and carried her petition to the Pope himself, with the result that the proceedings were brought to light and re-examined. From these meagre scraps we are, I think, at liberty to deduce that Joan inherited on the one side her all-sufficient religious faith, and from the other the single-mindedness that gives the power to surmount obstacles by simply ignoring them.

The position of the village of Domrémy is interesting to note, for it lay across the border of the Duchy of Lorraine, of which the reigning Duke was an ally of Burgundy. In spite of this it was fiercely loyal to free France, and the village children would sally forth with stones for a scrap with the children of other nearby villages that were known to be Burgundian in allegiance. The fighting that had rolled back and forth across Northern France had not really touched Domrémy, though it had suffered from isolated raids when the villagers, forewarned, drove their herds into the woods. But on the whole the life of the village was uneventful, nor were the peasants oppressed by a grasping feudal lord as was so often the case. It is true that the villagers of Domrémy and its neighbour Greux yearly scraped together a sum of money exacted in return for protection of their property by a local *Damoiseau* or Esquire, but it could not be called an exorbitant tax.

The river Meuse looped and threaded its way through that green valley much as it does today. In one place the stream divided, forming an island upon which stood an untenanted castle with a walled courtyard, the property of the local great family, the de Bourlemonts, but long fallen into disuse. Into this stronghold the villagers drove their cattle in unquiet times, and in and out of its crumbling bastions the children of the village, Joan among them, played at the age-old games of childhood, taking turns as to who should storm the breach and who should hold it.

For those of us who are not likely to see with our own eyes the cradle of Joan's childhood, Andrew Lang has beautifully described it: 'The straggling river, broken by little isles, and fringed with reeds, flows clear in summer; the chub and dace may be seen through its pellucid water, unbroken as it is by the dimples of the rising trout. As in a Hampshire chalk-stream the long green tresses of the water-weeds wave and float, the banks are gardens of water-flowers, the meadows are fragrant with meadow-sweet.'[1]

Since Joan's lifetime the river has changed its course, the house which tradition assigns to the family of Arc has been restored out of recognition. In her day this part of the country was almost all forest land; the flat buttercup fields along the river edge providing pasture for the village flocks. It is not a rich agricultural country, but it yielded a respectable living for

[1] *The Maid of France*, by Andrew Lang.

the sixty-odd families that made up the population of Domrémy and Greux.

From the time that she was old enough to be treated as a responsible person, Joan had to take her share in the work of the farm. Her life cannot have been gay, but no doubt it was absorbing as country life is in all climes and ages. She must have shivered under her rough frieze cloak, and wrapped her arms round her body for warmth on dripping autumn mornings in the fields, and learnt with pain to walk barefoot in the woods, bruising her feet on roots and stones.

At her Trial her inquisitors made much of a certain tree that stood in the dark wood on a slope above the village, called to this day the *Bois Chenu*; the oakwood, or the ancient wood. It had a sinister reputation, for it was the haunt of wild boar and wolves, and popularly believed to be the dancing ground of the fairies. The tree in question stood alone by a spring which was thought to possess healing properties. Bits of rag were stuck about on the bushes nearby by sick people who came to drink of it, as a sort of propitiation to the fairy legend which no one thought of disbelieving. Round this tree, which was called the Ladies' Tree, the children danced sometimes, and hung up wreaths of sorrel and daisies, no doubt with a daring sense of doing something of which their elders would not approve. All this was to look terribly black in the process of Joan's condemnation by the Church.

The truth was that to most peasants the border line between religion and ancient superstition was shadowy. The legends of the Christian faith that appealed most were those that touched a core of common humanity in all alike. The Saints, who had humanly suffered and been divinely rewarded, were the bright constant companions of the poor peasant, who in his sorrowful darkness craved for that touch of suffering kinship. These took the places of the old kindly gods of the woods, who, though displaced, were not quite forgotten. A peasant driving his pigs through the *Bois Chenu* in search of fodder, finding himself near the sacred tree, might, unthinking, jerk his hat off with an involuntary gesture of homage. Joan, after the revelation had come to her, took no more share in the pagan revels of her companions, but that may well have been because the heavy secret she carried weighed on her and disinclined her feet for dancing.

While the elders of the village worked at the sowing and tilling and reaping of their acres, their children took turns in driving the herds out to pasture. Joan took her turn with the rest, but, on her own admission, having made sure that none of the cows or sheep were likely to stray, she often played truant.

In the heart of the woods was a little whitewashed shrine, no bigger than a hut, dedicated to Notre Dame de Bermont. To get to it was quite a long climb and a lonely one. Yet she braved the danger of wolves, and the greater terrors, to a childish mind, of silence and solitude, to kneel before the crude wooden figure of the Virgin, which stands to this day. Her hour had not yet struck, but the breathless awe of it was upon her. Of that silent communing in the deserted chapel she told no one.

One day in summer—the year was 1424, and the English had just won another notable victory at Verneuil, after a summer of unbroken military successes—Joan and her companions were running races in a meadow while the sheep cropped near at hand. She was now nearly thirteen, almost a woman, and well grown for her age. Her heart for the moment being light, she ran lightly, seeming to her companions not to touch the ground with her feet. Having won with ease, she flung herself down among the long grasses to pant and recover. There are varying versions of this story, but all are agreed that while thus resting, someone came up to her and told her that she was wanted at home. This 'someone' is unidentifiable, and Joan herself said that she thought it was one of the boys of the village. Her mother was in the house, and seeing her daughter returning, called out in a scolding voice to ask why she had left the sheep which she was supposed to be minding. Bewildered, the girl turned back.

It was the time of day when the sun is at its height and shadows are shortest. It was hot and Joan had eaten nothing that day, so that with the exertion of the race she may well have felt dazzled and faint.

In her own words she has described how she saw on her right hand a strong light that was of a different quality from the leaf-chequered sunshine all round her. Her first reaction was pure terror. But the voice that presently came out of that terrible brightness was deep and kind. It told her in simple words that there was nothing to be afraid of, and that she was a good child and must continue to be devout and obedient. By the time her knees had stopped trembling the brightness had quite faded, and the light of common day possessed her eyes again. Her own simple words convey the scene; *'I was in my thirteenth year when God sent a voice to guide me. At first I was very much frightened. The voice came toward the hour of noon, in summer in my father's garden. . . .'*

It was a shattering enough experience for helpless immaturity to cope with and set in proportion. But Joan, even at the age of thirteen, was not immature; from earliest childhood she had lived with the realities of country life, death from lingering sickness; poverty in its crudest form; birth. Nor was she helpless; those hours alone in the hushed stillness of the chapel in the wood had filled her to the brim with peace—all

47

her short life she drew on that inexhaustible source of assurance, and at the end it did not fail her.

It is not possible that news of the latest English victory had filtered through to Domrémy, for the battle of Verneuil was fought in August 1424, and Joan speaks of 'midsummer' as the time of her first revelation. It is hardly likely that the rumour of a defeat so distant could have thrown her into the morbid condition in which she might have imagined the bright light and the Voice among the branches of her father's apple trees. Later, after the command had come, bidding her go forth and do battle for her country, she asserted emphatically that she would rather have been torn in pieces than attempt such a thing on her own account, involving, as it must have done, disobedience to her parents, and immodest exhibition of herself in the company of soldiers, whom she had very rightly been brought up to shun. Never for a moment did Joan betray any of the symptoms of the exhibitionist, of the sufferer from delusions, or of the mentally unstable.

The vision came again and with time she lost her fear of it. It came sometimes at night, but most often in the silence of noon in the woods, or in the fields at evening, when the church bells of all the villages dotted up and down the valley were ringing. At first it was no more than a voice speaking *très bien et bellement* out of a luminous cloud. But in a little it began to assume personality and to be recognizable to the child's senses as St. Michael, the Archangel. Afterwards she could never be got to describe him. To what extent the vision conformed to the popular medieval conception of a fighting archangel—i.e. a being in shining armour, with flowing yellow hair, and great wings folded about him—we do not know. We only know that Joan soon had no more doubt of his identity, though at first she had been in great fear that it might be all a trick, or a visitation from the Devil.

He spoke always gently and comfortingly, but with increasing authority. He spoke of the sufferings of France till the child wept, and led her inexorably to the contemplation of her own destiny. She was the daughter of God and it was His command that she should put on man's dress and carry arms like a man for the salvation of her country, and in the service of the true King. 'Go forward,' said the Saint, 'and all things shall be ordered by your counsel.'

It is hardly possible to believe that no one noticed a change in her. When questioned many years after her death, the old people of the village shook their heads. One child among so many! No one had particularly remarked her, though one or two recalled that she bowed and crossed herself when the church bells rang for vespers; but that in itself was not remarkable. We know that from the first visitation she shunned the rowdier of her companions, and withdrew into herself. If her mother noticed anything she probably put it down to the growing-pains of adolescence.

This was to go on for four years. Besides the Archangel, St. Margaret and St. Catherine visited her. They became her friends and the companions of her lonely days and nights. Always they encouraged and calmed her with the blessed assurance that she would, when the time came, be upheld and strengthened by God, whose daughter she was.

After these encounters she would sigh at finding herself alone, and then weep for the sorrows of France that before had seemed like a distant rumour from another world. Already the tears of humanity had touched her simple, hardy youth. At home in the house of Jacques d'Arc she sat silent at her father's table, her ears singing and her eyes burning with the unimaginable beauty of her Saints, and in her heart pity for the whole world.

Chapter Three

The First Journey

IF a labourer's daughter of today were miraculously commanded to arm herself and go into battle, it would not be so difficult for her to get a sympathetic hearing. But even today Kings and Governments do not accord audiences to loud-voiced peasants who come riding with a motley following. In the fifteenth century it was unthinkable that a woman should have a voice in any matter relevant to the State, unless she were placed by the accident of birth in a position to wield influence; such a woman was the Queen-mother, Isabelle of France, such a woman was Yolande of Sicily, mother-in-law of the Dauphin.

But between these royal ladies and poor Joan was a great gulf. To anyone less sure, the obstacles must have seemed insurmountable. But Joan had strength of character above the average. Not only did she lock that burning secret in her heart for nearly four years, but when the hour struck she did not draw back or waver. One can argue that she lacked sophistication, or that the almost daily converse with her Saints had so exalted her that she hardly perceived the practical difficulties ahead. But Joan at her most exalted was always practical; and her lack of sophistication did not prevent her from mixing with the great of the land, or joining in their conversation with a complete unawareness of social barriers that must have made their condescension appear both stilted and silly.

It is not difficult to form a picture of Joan, though no pictorial likeness has come down to us that is reliable. We know that her hair was black and that it hung down long and thick, and that in build she was sturdy and tall. She had a deep voice, and when giving an order could effortlessly make herself heard some distance away. Chroniclers who never saw her have affirmed that she was as beautiful as she was pious. Some of her biographers have been too ready to believe this, witness Andrew Lang's idealized portrait of her:

'Her hair was black, cut short like a soldier's; as to eyes and features, having no information, we may conceive of them as we please. Probably she had grey eyes, and a clear, pale colour under the tan of sun and wind. She was so tall that she could wear men's clothes. Thus, with her natural aspect of gladness and her ready April tears, Jeanne was a maid whom men loved to look upon and followed gladly . . . In Chaucer's pretty phrase she was: "Sweet as a flower and upright as a bolt." '

There is at least one error here; Joan inspired men, but not with love. There is no evidence of that, but plenty to the contrary; she could be in the company of the roughest soldiers all day, and at night sleep amongst them without provoking in them any sexual feeling. When she adopted men's clothes it provided her with sexual immunity; short-haired, tunicked, booted like the rest, she became as one of them.

Romantic love in those days was a sort of convention; it was the fashion. We can imagine that courtly affectations of gallantry must have moved Joan to contempt. In Domrémy women married and grew worn and prematurely old in the struggle against poverty, weather, and sickness. Marriage was a social contract in which both man and woman fulfilled their part. The exaggerated deference which it was the fashion for knights and nobles of the Court to show to ladies must have faltered before Joan's surprised disgust. Carrying her inspiration, like a lamp in her breast, she knew only one kind of love, the love of God. For mankind that suffered and had no voice, she had unbounded and beautiful compassion; but there is no evidence that in her brief span she ever loved after humanity's pattern.

I see her against the shifting tapestry of her short life, a peasant in build and feature. Those chill autumn mornings, those sharp spring evenings, had made of her something tough and resilient, as the sun had browned her strong arms and sturdy legs till they had the look of young trees. I find it difficult to imagine that there can have been anything flower-like about Joan, but a kind of beauty there may have been, as of a strongly-rooted freely-growing plant. Her features were most probably flat and broad, with the eyes perhaps set in deep bone sockets; such faces are still bred out of the soil of Lorraine. The deep, musical voice that many of her contemporaries commented on must have come from a well-built body, and her exhibition of endurance in the saddle speaks of splendid health and great muscular strength.

She had had no education beyond a stringent and pious upbringing. She could not sign her own name. But she could spin and cook expertly and in these matters was her mother's right hand. She was proud to brag of it after she had quitted her father's roof for ever. Joan in shining armour, the friend of princes, the adored of the French populace, was always ineradicably the peasant's child of Domrémy. Not the least remarkable thing about her was the way in which, when flattery of the grossest kind was being lavished on her, she kept her head as well as her sound country standards of behaviour.

In 1428 Joan reached the age of sixteen and was officially considered to have grown up. All this time she had been silent on the subject of her visions, going about her household and farm duties, webbed in a dream from which she would presently wake to reality. If we accept, as we must accept, the miracle that had happened to her, then we must believe that she was miraculously sustained through those four years of silence. It would have been such a relief to tell someone, such sweet self-indulgence and respite! But while her Saints forbade it, her lips were locked.

She was now of an age to be sought in marriage. It is probable that her parents saw some indefinable difference in her that worried them, and wished to see her settled and housebound. Jacques d'Arc had dreamed more than once that he saw his girl riding away in the company of armed men, and that could mean only one thing. Most fathers would there and then have taken a strap and given their daughters a sound beating as a deterrent to loose behaviour. But Jacques d'Arc, eyeing his daughter strangely, said nothing of it to anyone but his wife, though later he is reported to have told his sons that if they saw their sister going with the soldiers they were to drown her in the river, or, if they would not, he would.

In the meanwhile the English had recruited another army at home and this, under the Earl of Salisbury, was preparing to besiege the city of Orléans, held by the Bastard of Orléans, illegitimate son of the murdered Duke Louis.

With this, the third city of France, in their hands, the English could control the Loire and be in a strategic position to blockade the Dauphin's territory.

The voices of St. Michael, St. Catherine, and St. Margaret spoke to Joan with bell-like insistence. The hour was near when she was to deceive her parents and bid farewell for ever to the friends of her youth. France was in grave danger, the blood of slain Frenchmen called to her, and the stifled voices of the living implored redress. Joan wept—tears came easily to her—and then in her practical way set about finding a reason for leaving home which would not be likely to rouse her parents' suspicions.

A cousin on her mother's side had married a labourer called Durand Lassois and lived only two miles from the garrison town of Vaucouleurs, which was held in the name of the Dauphin. The Governor of this town, de Baudricourt, was not unknown to Jacques d'Arc, so that Joan had probably heard his name mentioned, and also that he was a rough and hardy soldier, and loyal to the cause of France. It was simple to persuade her mother that her cousin Lassois needed help about the house. She was allowed to go on a week's visit.

It was not quite so simple to persuade her 'uncle,' Durand, that she had a mission from God to Robert de Baudricourt in his castle at Vaucouleurs and that it was his duty to conduct her thither. However, persuade him she did. She was artful enough—there was a streak of innocent guile in Joan—to play on his ignorance and credulity with legends that were current in that part of the country concerning a maid from the Marches of Lorraine who would rise up and save France. There was another old tale that Merlin, the arch-enchanter, had foretold that Domrémy would breed a maid for the healing of her distressed nation. Durand Lassois was a simple man, not easily shaken out of his plodding ways. He saw in Joan a well-grown girl, with bare feet and hands, brown as hazel nuts, and a thick rope of black hair, wearing a faded gown of handspun crimson stuff. She did not look at all like the saviour of France, but like every other peasant girl of her age. But he gave in; it was the first triumph for Joan's strong, compelling personality.

Robert de Baudricourt was not impressed. He soon whistled the prophecies of Merlin and the testament of angels down the wind, and advised that Joan be taken back to her father to be given the beating she deserved, or alternatively he suggested handing her over to the pleasure of his men-at-arms. Lassois hastily removed his troublesome young relation, who returned to her father's house, not visibly cast down by the failure of this initial attempt.

There is no record of what Jacques d'Arc said when his daughter returned home. There must have been talk, and curious glances must have followed the girl as she went about her duties. It may be that what had passed confirmed the father in his secret misgivings—he had had those disturbing dreams about her.

The English pressure in the North had repercussions about this time (July 1428) on the borders of Lorraine. Antoine de Vergy, the governor of Champagne, determined to subjugate on his own the pro-French neighbourhood of Vaucouleurs, and all the villages along that part of the Meuse valley. The villagers hurriedly bundled up all their goods, their clothes and dishes and poor sticks of furniture, lumped them on farm carts, and with their cattle streamed out of Domrémy in a southerly direction to the town of Neufchâteau. Had the rumour been simply of a foraging raid they would, as they had often done before, have driven their livestock into the Chateau de l'Isle already referred to, till the danger was passed.

The villagers of that valley were hardy and independent. Their spirits had not been sapped by the cynical tyranny of a feudal princeling. That strip of country had remained stubbornly pro-Dauphin, in spite of its proximity to Burgundian territory. The devastation that had visited the rest of France had spared Domrémy, and the villagers had listened hard-mouthed and unimpressed to the tales carried by vagrant priests and deserters from both sides who sought shelter there. De Vergy's threat to their peace was formidable enough to shake them from the rut of complacent indifference.

To the child and the growing girl Joan, who, first from an inconspicuous seat in the chimney corner, and later from her kitchen duties and while waiting upon strangers, listened silently, tales of the English occupation must have sounded like rumours of another world. After her Voices had spoken, she realized that this was the world for which she must leave the narrow, peaceful place where she was loved and known.

When the village hurriedly packed up and departed to Neufchâteau, Joan may have looked back as the dust rose in their wake, to impress on her mind the details of a scene she might never see again. War had come suddenly very close.

While at Neufchâteau, Joan became most strangely and inexplicably involved in a breach of promise case with a young man from Toul; she appeared before a court in Toul and told them indignantly that she had never given her word that she would marry anyone. The case was dismissed. The incident is unimportant except that it counted as one more nail in her coffin when the judges at her trial were industriously raking up every small incident that might tell against her. This episode frightened her, no doubt. While under her father's roof she must be in the humiliating and dependent

59

position of a child. Now she was in disgrace as well, and perpetually under the anxious, reproachful eye of her parents, to whom she was unwilling to give pain.

That autumn of 1428 was spent busily in carting stones for the rebuilding of the village; for the troopers of Antoine de Vergy had left it desolate and smoke-blackened. The church into which Joan had often crept to pray unobserved was roofless and windowless.

Salisbury had landed in France in July with an army, and after taking, as a preliminary, several towns along the Loire, settled down to besiege the city of Orléans.

By October news had filtered through that Orléans was surrounded by the English. Joan heard it as a premonition that the hour was about to strike. Her Voices had foretold it. She made up her mind that her next visit to Robert de Baudricourt should take place in the New Year; again the Lassois' would be useful to her, as her cousin was due to have a baby about then. She was impatient to be gone, for the suspense of waiting was unnerving. She was very young and for four years had lived as a stranger under her father's roof, conscious in every nerve of her growing body of the thrilling destiny promised her. Silence, respect, obedience, must have been as irksome to her as a curb to a mettlesome, strong pony.

It is hard to understand why, with the affair

of her last visit to Vaucouleurs in their minds, her parents should have let her go a second time. It is recorded that as the time drew near she seemed unusually gay, and even relaxed her vow of reticence, with half sentences of strange meaning flung casually to her companions. The reason for her going, her usefulness to the Lassois household, was unassailable. We may suppose that some forewarning of her great destiny struck Jacques and Isabelle d'Arc silent, or that Durand Lassois had communicated to them something of the spell Joan had cast on him. At all events they let her go with bitter tears and clinging. The villagers stood silent at their doors as she rode away behind her uncle under a low, threatening January sky; one or two waved and answered her greeting.

Many, many years later, when testimony was required of them that should rehabilitate Joan as the starry-eyed, heaven-graced prodigy of the village, these men and women, grown old, racked their dimmed brains for some recollection to oblige. But all they could personally remember of the headstrong daughter of Jacques d'Arc was that she was a good child, gentle and pious. Much like other children.

Robert de Baudricourt was not a patient man. His position as Governor of Vaucouleurs was an anxious one; he could rarely extend himself to repose in the conviction that all was well within

the borders of his domain. Vaucouleurs was a
frontier town in the shadow of Burgundy, and
the recent—as it turned out, unsuccessful—punitive
expedition of Antoine de Vergy had frightened
the townspeople and done a lot of expensive
damage. All day long he sat in his great hall
behind a table, listening to petitions and com-
plaints. An endless procession filed through the
hall: farmers with grievances; peasants requiring
compensation for war damage (which had to be
proved); endless grumbling about the taxes it
was his duty to collect in the King's name; one
and all receiving the same flat, blunt treatment,
for he was the type of man who prided himself
on standing no nonsense. We can imagine what
must have been his feelings when out of the
procession of petitioners Durand Lassois stepped
forward, turning his cap in his poor, worn hands,
and, for the second time, stammeringly presented
his niece Joan.

There she stood in her patched gown, with the
same look of bright, impudent assurance that had
so riled him before. If Robert de Baudricourt
had smacked his fist down on to the table so that
the inkhorns leapt, and roared dismissal, no one
would have been surprised, least of all Durand
Lassois, who would think in his humble way
that the gentry probably knew best.

But Robert de Baudricourt was worried; the
news of the siege of Orléans was extremely disquieting. He had kept Vaucouleurs for the

rightful King of France by having an astute head on his shoulders, but if Orléans were to fall, and the English and Burgundian armies to pour across the Loire, no amount of astuteness would keep his head from being struck off with an English axe.

Perceiving his unease and hesitation Joan made the best of it. As far as we know she stayed six weeks in or near Vaucouleurs. Duly she assisted at the arrival of her cousin's baby, and later stayed with a wheelwright called Henry le Royer and his wife, Catherine. In between whiles she persistently haunted de Baudricourt in his castle, with the reiterated request to be sent to Chinon where her King was. He might storm at her and call her a brat and a hussy, or rudely refuse to listen, Joan remained calm and undaunted, serene with assurance that God and His Saints were with her.

She was not without earthly allies, too; two young men, captains in de Baudricourt's own garrison company, had ranged themselves on her side. Their names were Bertrand of Poulengy and John of Metz. Bertrand was noble by birth, but being poor like so many cadets of good family, had adopted war as a profession and lived the rough life of a mercenary soldier, scarcely distinguishable from the rest. John of Metz, though not noble, was a man of property, a small *seigneur*. It is recorded that, hearing of her—for she was by now the talk of the little crowded town of Vaucouleurs—he came to the wheelwright's house one night and spoke to her with gentleness, not with insulting roughness. Recognizing some quality of truth and reliability in him that she could rely on, Joan poured out her private disappointment. To de Baudricourt she had seemed impudently assured; but she was still a child and accustomed to accept the judgment of her elders and betters. She was discouraged by the delay—here we have a foreshadowing of her awareness that her time was to be terribly brief—'he takes scant notice of me, yet before Lent is half through I must be on my way to the King, if I wear my legs to my knees. There is no other person in the world, nor King nor duke, nor the daughter of the King of Scotland[1], nor any other, who can regain the Kingdom of France. . . .'

John of Metz perceived that she was truthful. 'I would rather be spinning by my mother's side,' said poor Joan, 'for these things do not belong to my station; yet it is necessary I should go and do these things, since God wishes that I should do them.'

John was moved by her sincerity and her tears and there and then pledged his faith to her, and said he would go with her, God helping them both, to the King. He shut his mind to the dangers of the journey, with an impetuosity

[1] The little daughter of James I of Scotland who was contracted in marriage to the Dauphin's young son. Part of her dowry was to be 6,000 archers: unfortunately they never materialized.

that did his honest heart credit, and offered to fit her up in the costume of one of his servants that she might travel unmolested the two hundred and fifty miles that lay between Vaucouleurs and Chinon where the Dauphin held court.

De Poulengy accepted her with the same unreserve as John of Metz had done. Men in those days were groping for truth and avid for miracles. The Church taught that the coming of Christ had let in light on a world of darkness, but it was plain to see that the world still seethed with injustices, and the blood of the oppressed flowed beneath the feet of the scornful. '. . . for over a thousand years the Church had been using the canonized dead as incarnations of the higher virtues and teaching that God's mercy was to be sought by their intercession.'[1] Therefore to the Saints men looked in pitiful eagerness, imploring some sign to show that they were not forgotten, not relegated to eternal punishment. Anything would do, no manifestation would be overlooked. Twigs and stones and streams to which some natural process had lent an unusual conformation became mystic and endowed with healing power. Fine harvest weather, a monster catch of herrings, a fever cured, a victory, all were sure proof that God was not unpitying and that His Saints kept vigil. To the poor towns-people of Vaucouleurs, Joan, with her heavenly confidence, was such a manifestation. They

[1] *Joan of Arc*, Milton Waldman.

welcomed her with simple gratitude as a sign
that God had not forgotten France.

When de Poulengy added his weight to that
of John of Metz, de Baudricourt was shaken;
but he had his position as Governor of the town
to consider. If the girl turned out to be a witch
or a fraud he would look a fine fool for intro-
ducing her to the notice of the Court. He was
astute enough to observe one or two things about
her: that her testimony never varied; that she
had convinced, without apparently resorting to
feminine wiles, two of his ablest captains; that
she had occupied herself diligently in the wheelwright's household, and did not hang about the
guard-room—in fact, the men-at-arms showed
uneasiness and embarrassment at his jovial
suggestion that he should turn her over to their
pleasure. (Yet she was not a bad-looking girl.)
He decided that the matter was out of his
province, and called in a priest.

The priest, one Fournier, had already heard
Joan's confession, but anxious to stand in well
with the Governor, he was ready to apply the
test of witchcraft which de Baudricourt required.
Together they visited le Royer's house, and
Fournier solemnly admonished Joan to keep
away from him if the spirit within her was evil.

The poor girl had already had some experience
of the stupidity and blindness of men; this was
her first encounter with the crooked-mindedness
of the Church, of which she was the submissive,

loving child. Hurt, she approached him on her knees, and in this lowly position asked his blessing. De Baudricourt, half expecting to see her shrivel up in smoke there and then, was rather disappointed. Joan was deeply outraged, and that night wept tears of indignation. But it did not occur to her to doubt her Voices. They had told that through de Baudricourt she would go to her King, and she did not question it.

But time was running on. To her hostess, Catherine le Royer, Joan said, thinking probably of her Lassois cousin's recent confinement, that the time seemed as long to her as to an expectant woman waiting for her deliverance.

Her impatience to be up and doing led her to set out on foot to Chinon, till her good sense persuaded her that such an arrival, dirty, ragged, and footsore, would not be likely to gain her an entrance at Court. But she did make an expedition that seems to us rather odd; to Nancy, to the Court of the Duke of Lorraine, an old man sick of a loathsome disease, who, hearing of the importunate girl who claimed to be the chosen of Heaven to save France from the English, sent for her to come and cure him.

We must remember that Joan was still new to the world outside Domrémy. Her bright, new-minted confidence in herself had not been dulled by her first encounter with official scepticism. The Duke's invitation must have raised her hopes that here was an alternative way, even though her Voices had not sanctioned such an expedient. If she could but convince this great and powerful prince, then de Baudricourt must believe in her. Anyway, it was unthinkable to disobey one's feudal lord, so she duly set out for Nancy on a borrowed horse, with the dog-like Durand Lassois as her escort.

But Charles of Lorraine, who had sent for her in a fit of idle curiosity, was no ally. He was one of the several vassal princes who had pledged themselves to abide by the terms of the Treaty of Troyes, and held his principality of Lorraine by favour of the Regent Bedford and the Duke of Burgundy. Joan, admitted for the first time to the splendour of a feudal Court, was not overawed. In her peasant's dress of crimson homespun, her feet bare, and with her black hair twisted into a rope, she stood squarely on the rich carpet before the Duke in his great chair. The haggard *bon viveur* had no interest for her: she saw at a glance that he would be no help to her. She told him roundly that she knew no cure for his malady save to abstain from evil living. If he would give her his son-in-law (and heir) and some fighting men to conduct her into France she would pray for his recovery. More than that she could not promise. There must have been something disarming about Joan's unrelenting truthfulness. At all events the Duke did not take offence. He gave her

some gold for the expenses of her journey and a
horse to return on and dismissed her.

In the meanwhile Robert de Baudricourt had
dispatched a letter to Chinon. As one chronicler
puts it, he had been *moult ennuyeusement prie* or
most tediously besought by the girl from Lorraine, and his resistance had been sapped.
Added to which he was much disturbed about
the conduct of the war. It looked as if only a
miracle could reinstate Charles VII on the
throne of France. Well, he had proved to his
own satisfaction that Joan was no witch. Let
her go and work the miracle, if she could. Like
Pilate, he wanted only to be allowed to wash
his hands of the whole business.

It is interesting that to no other man, save
only her King, did Joan speak of her Voices.
To her they were so dear and sacred, that she
could never bring herself to mention them.
Yet de Baudricourt was notoriously rude and
sceptical.

On her return from Nancy she went straight
to him, bursting in without ceremony, crying:
'In God's name you are too slow; for this day
near Orléans a great disaster has befallen our
gentle Dauphin, and worse fortune he will have
unless you send me to him.'

It was prophetic. A day or two later there
came news of the humiliation of the French and
Scots at Rouvray, when attacking an English
convoy that was carrying food to the army

besieging Orléans. The baggage wagons containing barrels of salted herrings, the staple of the army's Lenten fare, were scattered over the field. The news of this Battle of the Herrings came hard upon Joan's reproach, and at the same time as a letter from the Dauphin authorizing him to send the girl to Chinon.

All was rejoicing in Vaucouleurs. The townspeople insisted on having their share in the glory of the occasion. She must have a new outfit and they would provide it. It consisted of a wide tunic of thick wool, grey in colour, to be gathered in tightly at the waist with a leather belt. It had a high neck and hooked up under the chin. Over this went a sleeveless tunic of leather, dyed black, and laced up the front with leather thongs. Long grey woollen stockings, high boots of soft hide that fitted the leg, and a woollen cap with a long tail that wound round the head completed the travelling outfit of a page or esquire of the period.

The swinging rope of hair was shorn off close to her head. Strange and unfamiliar it must have felt to Joan to be unencumbered by that heavy mane and the clinging folds of her old red dress. This was the initial step, more significant, more final, than the leaving of home and childhood. It was also the most obvious common sense, for no woman could hope to travel unharmed through lawless country in the company of soldiers. John of Metz had realized that when he offered to dress her in the livery of his followers.

Joan, with her strong legs and shoulders and deep voice, made a passable boy. She had on one or two occasions borrowed the poor clothes of her faithful Durand Lassois. The step of changing herself into the guise of a page did not seem so fateful to her, since no other costume was practicable. At her trial she was impatient when accused of immodesty. Couldn't they see that it was expedient, the dolts and dunderheads who were always trying to confuse the essential with the unessential? Apparently they could not or would not; at the last it was the thing that brought her to the stake.

The Duke of Lorraine's horse was not considered good enough. The townspeople subscribed and bought her another, costing sixteen francs. Robert de Baudricourt gloomily—we imagine he cannot have shared the general jubilance—presented her with a sword. In character to the last moment, he sped the party with the words: 'Go, go! and come what may! (*Va, va! et advienne que pourra.*)

The little party—Joan leading, Bertrand of Poulengy and John of Metz following with their servants, the Dauphin's envoy, and a scattering of hangers-on—clattered out of Vaucouleurs on the darkening afternoon of February 23rd, 1429. They were to travel by night for greater safety. The people had crowded about her stirrups with wistful, anxious faces, concerned for the safety of this chosen child of Heaven. But she, looking ahead, saw only the end and bothered not all about the means. 'The way lies clear before me,' she serenely told them when they spoke of the dangers. 'If I meet them I have God, who makes smooth the road to my lord the King. For to do this deed was I born. . . .'

After the crowd had dispersed and the echo of horses' hoofs died away into silence, Durand Lassois must have stood gazing after the dwindling figure in the grey and black tunics. I think it is legitimate to picture him thus. His life had been, and would be again, poor and humdrum. But a thread of scarlet had been worked into it. He had experienced, through his young cousin by marriage, enchantment and exaltation, as well as worry and alarm. He had been in his small way, and for a brief period, the instrument of God.

Chapter Four

Joan and the King

TO get to Chinon it was necessary to pass through Burgundian territory, and it must have been an anxious business for the men accompanying Joan to shepherd their charge through hostile country. Joan alone was unconcerned. Her calm was unshaken by their evident uneasiness. Many times did de Poulengy and John of Metz question her anxiously if she was really as certain as she seemed that all would be well; to which came the invariable steady answer: 'Fear not, what I do is by command.'

Neither of them was a rich man, and they had financed this undertaking without hope of ever seeing any of their money back. Neither can have had a very clear idea of what awaited them at the end of their journey. All that she prophesied they had to take on trust. As soldiers they knew, better than she could imagine, the dangers that prowled in the waste lands through which they must pass. They had a personal pride in her; she was their discovery and their liability. De Baudricourt had made it clear before they left that he was not going to be held responsible. His letter to the Dauphin had been worded guardedly. If the holy maid of Domrémy turned out to be neither miraculous nor a virgin, he would have them remember that he had had his doubts about her from the first.

They travelled mostly by night, when the faint stars hardly lightened the encompassing dark. Flood-water stood in the fields and made the going heavy. By day they kept to the shelter of woods and snatched their sleep there, deep in the leafless scrub. Joan would wrap her woollen cloak tightly about her and sleep in all her clothes, not even loosening the high boots of soft hide that were laced to the hem of her jerkin.

John of Metz simply records that such was his respect for her that he never was aware of any evil desires, even when they lay close together for warmth. Yet he and de Poulengy were young men, and their experience as soldiers cannot have inclined them to scrupulousness or delicacy where women of a lower class were concerned. It is probable that they had, in common with the rest of a licentious age, a fanatical respect for virginity. Without it, all Joan's inspiration from her Saints would have carried no weight. As a virgin she could claim miraculous powers (though she never did). As de Poulengy afterwards declared, he would never have dared make her an evil suggestion because of the virtue he divined in her. Joan, while trusting whole-heartedly in the promise of her Voices that no

bodily harm should come to her, was sensible
enough not to put temptation in their way.

The alarm and uncertainty that her companions constantly showed must have been
discouraging. But we are told that nothing
distressed Joan but the fact that, owing to the
dangers of the road, the little band had to travel
furtively, and were not able to stop and hear Mass
as often as she wished. It took eleven or twelve
days to get from Vaucouleurs to Chinon. On the
way they paused at the hospitable Abbey of
St. Urbain, and at the shrine of St. Catherine of
Fierbois where Joan prayed long and fervently
to the dearest of her Saints.

How tired her escorts must have become of
scanning the landscape for stray bands of robbers
—for even after leaving Burgundian territory
there was always danger of falling into the hands
of prowling soldiery who might hold them for
ransom. And what relief it was to see the grey
walls of Chinon towering out of the flooded fields
of Touraine. It was by now the first week of
March and there was a loosening feeling of spring
in the air. Joan's spirits rose with every mile.

For most of the journey she had been silenced
by the desolation that lay all about them. It has
been said that the valley of the Meuse had not
been visited by war: the raids of local barons,
financed by Burgundy, had passed over it and
done some damage, but left the face of the country
unchanged. To travellers' tales of the devastation

'up North' the villagers had pursed their mouths. Joan was well acquainted with the facts and rigours of country life at its barest and most uncompromising. But the spartan decency of her upbringing had not prepared her for sights such as she now saw. Strewn on all sides were ruins of farms, with doors hanging on one hinge, their sheds and stables gaping empty under smoke-blackened thatch. By the roadside were bones and carcases of beasts that had died of neglect or been slaughtered by the freebooters for food. It was rare to see smoke curling from a chimney, or washing hanging on a line, or a field under cultivation. The pity for humanity that was in Joan's heart brimmed and overflowed. For this she had been born: to restore peace to this torn land. Her eyes were often blind with tears as she rode, but this she was careful to keep from her companions.

In the castle of Chinon there was a mild stir of expectation; De Baudricourt's letter had guaranteed nothing. The girl might be inspired or she might not. In the grudging opinion of the Governor of Vaucouleurs she was genuine, but the Dauphin and his Ministers must be the best judges of that.

The deadly monotony of Court life made the Dauphin's entourage ready to welcome any spectacle. And an inspired virgin, though not exactly a novelty in those days, would be sure to provide their sophistication with entertainment, such as they derived from watching the pathetic near-human antics of a pet monkey. They crowded the hall, peering over each other's shoulders. With their monstrous sleeves, and shoes a yard long, and with the women's enormous padded headdresses like the horns of demented heifers, it was they who looked sub-human. When a page banged on the floor and announced Joan's arrival, all faces were turned one way and the gale of chatter stilled. As she stepped into the great hall of Chinon, lit with torches, flaming and smoking high up on the walls, Joan must have received a confused impression of kaleidoscopic brilliance. There were, beside the Prince, the head of the Army, the Duke de la Trémoille, and Regnault de Chartres, Archbishop of Rheims and Primate of France. She took it all in, we may be sure, standing squarely in her shabby grey and black. She had already had some experience of grandeur from her visit to the Duke of Lorraine. As for the courtiers' scarcely-suppressed smiles, she was unaware of them. In her calm, common-sense fashion she sized them up and dismissed them for what they were, a lot of idle, greedy hangers-on, with nothing to do but keep their hands white. She brushed them aside like a cloud of gnats and strode up the hall.

Charles the Dauphin had received de Baudricourt's letter with mixed feelings. He was an unhappy man, conscious of his own inability to rise to his destiny. With one half of himself he wanted only to be allowed to sink into comfortable obscurity. Yet in his fretful, feeble way he craved also to do the thing that was right, and something inside him that would not let him rest whispered that he was slandered, that the blood of Valois ran in his veins, the blood of his wise, statesmanlike grandfather, Charles V. His mother's careless avowal of his illegitimacy was like a thorn under his skin. The situation, political and military, could not have been worse. God had forgotten or was bent on punishing France. Charles was religious, in a nervous, superstitious way; but like all weaklings he besieged the ear of Heaven with hysterical petitions for a miracle, instead of bestirring his own flabby brain and sinews.

Joan had not been admitted to the royal presence immediately on arrival at Chinon. She had already experienced teasing delay at Vaucouleurs while de Baudricourt made up his unready mind; from now on she was to learn that the earthly path of the visionary is an uphill one, and for every step taken she was to slide back two.

The 'defeatist' party at Court was led by the Dauphin's disagreeable favourite, the Duke de la Trémoille. This nobleman had a shady past, he came of a family of Burgundian sympathies, had more than one political murder on his conscience, and was now battening on the Dauphin's weak dependence on him. That he was enormously stout all the records agree; he would shake like a huge jelly with joviality, while his little eyes gave nothing away. His royal master, who feared him because he owed him money, he alternately bullied and cajoled. His policy was 'risk nothing.' He wanted no inspired peasant girl to teach him how to run the army, and said so roundly.

It is probable that it was the influence of his mother-in-law, the Queen of Sicily, on top of de Baudricourt's letter that broke down Charles' caution. Yolande of Sicily was a sensible woman, and saw the reins of power being twitched out of her son-in-law's flaccid grasp by unscrupulous men. This girl from Lorraine had three honourable soldiers to vouch for her and had already shown tenacity of purpose above the average. She claimed to have been chosen to crown the Dauphin at Rheims—if she could do that it would be half-way to winning the country over from the English. Though she was reputed homely of appearance she had some gift for drawing men to her side. It would do no harm to accord her an interview.

Charles was at last shaken out of his apathy. He gave the order to let the girl come in. But, fearing to be made a fool of, he dived behind a knot of courtiers when Joan was announced, and, peering over someone else's shoulder, watched her unembarrassed progress up the hall. Now if she were truly sent by Heaven, let her prove it!

What followed is well known. Joan wasted not a glance on the brocaded throng about her, or at the laughing young man who had seated himself in the Prince's chair, but went straight to where Charles hid, and, bobbing a country curtsey, said in her clear voice: 'Gentle Prince, they call me Joan the Maid. The King of Heaven has sent me to you. . . .'

The crowd, murmuring, fell away and left them face to face. Some emanation from Joan seems to have touched Charles then. He seized her hands and drew her apart into his private Chapel. What they said to one another is not known. Some secret passed between them; most likely she confirmed that he was indeed of the House of Valois and true-begotten son of his father. According to Joan's own testimony her Voices had promised her that when she found herself in her sovereign's presence she would be empowered to give him some sign by which he would know she was from God. But this was admitted under pressure at her Trial, and the rather garbled story of an angel with a golden crown that appeared to the two of them sounds like reckless invention. We have no dependable clue as to the nature of the sign. It seems possible that Joan, in her single-mindedness of purpose, by telepathic divination saw into his mind and laid bare the secret, hidden misgiving that tormented him. Some rumour of it may already have reached her, though this seems unlikely.

Though such a rumour may have been current at Court, it would hardly have penetrated as far

as Domrémy, and would have been indignantly
disbelieved if it had. Joan's passionate loyalty
ennobled the swollen features, the watery eyes,
and all the weakness and timidity he displayed in
his associations with her. To her he was God's
lieutenant on earth. Nothing, not English or
Burgundian might, nor the ill-will of his enemies
and detractors, could take that holy inheritance
from him.

Whatever passed between them it was noticed
when they rejoined the company that his face had
a brighter aspect and that he seemed to have
gained an inch in stature. To the amazement of
everyone he ordered that she was to be lodged in
a tower of the castle. La Trémoille might
crimson like a turkey cock, but for once Charles
ignored his favourite's bluster.

Joan, perceiving in her loving blindness nothing
but gentleness and truth in him, must have found
it hard to understand his subsequent behaviour.
A swing back into irritating caution was characteristic of Charles. The glow that had been reflected
from her and had warmed him with like
enthusiasm soon cooled; there was no spark to
kindle a flame in that small, cold heart of his.

She was treated with respect, if respect had been
what she wanted. Her lodging was in the Tour de
Coudray. She was given a page to wait on her,
whose testimony in after years, though often
inaccurate, presents us with sharply-edged
glimpses of her. This boy, whose name was

Louis de Contes, was only a few years younger than herself. It was the fashion for youth of rank to receive a courtly training in this way. She shared with him her restlessness at delay and her homesickness for the sweet air of the Meuse valley, as if he were one of her own brothers. He often watched her praying, and saw the tears rain down her face.

She was virtually a prisoner and might not come and go at will. This first taste of honourable captivity fretted her, but she schooled herself to be patient. Matrons of the Court visited her for the purpose of discovering if she really was a female; famous men came to question her. She was fed from the Dauphin's table. It all must have seemed very unreal to her. Daily she was closeted with the Dauphin, and her calm assurances that it was God's Will he should be crowned at Rheims turned into urgent exhortations to waste no more valuable time but send her with an army to relieve Orléans before it was too late.

She had her partisans, a growing number. Since her ride from Vaucouleurs, wonderful enough in itself, considering the dangers of the way, there had been other signs. Her recognition of the Dauphin was acclaimed as one; another instance of her power of divination had taken place as she rode up the entry of the Castle. An unidentified person, perhaps a man-at-arms, seeing her, called out coarsely, with an oath, that if he could have her for a night he would not return her a maid. 'In the name of God,' said Joan, 'dare you blaspheme and you so near to your end?' Whether she intended this as an actual prophecy, we shall never know; the man, at all events, was drowned in the moat that same night. The story was told by her confessor Pasquerel at the trial for the Rehabilitation of the Maid.

Besides Louis de Contes who haunted her like a little dog, Joan had made another friend. The young Duke d'Alençon seems to have been one of the select few who recognized Joan's quality as soon as they set eyes on her. Joan took him to her heart from the first. He was the son-in-law of the Duke of Orléans who had been dug out from under a pile of slain men at Agincourt, and sent as a prisoner over to England, there to write wistful verse in praise of youth and spring. Joan, in her ignorance, had never read '*le temps à laissé son manteau, de vent, de froidure, et de pluie*,' but the image would have appealed to her. She loved young d'Alençon for what he was, a soldier, a sportsman, a fine horseman, a gay companion, and for being the son-in-law of the poet Duke, whose name was a legend to his countrymen. They tilted together after dinner in the water meadows below the Castle, and d'Alençon, impressed by her easy mastery of the lance, made her a present of a horse.

This time it was a horse to be proud of; not

a farm horse such as the one on which she had ridden away from home behind Durand Lassois, or a travelling hack such as the Duke of Lorraine had given her. The horse which de Baudricourt and the townspeople of Vaucouleurs had sub-scribed those sixteen francs for had been well enough; it had carried her faithfully over two hundred and fifty miles of rough going to Chinon. But this was a horse of mettle, trained to respond to the lightest touch. It was part of the battle equipment of a knight, and Joan's heart lifted at the prospect of riding it against the English.

But Charles' caution grew with her impatience. He was ready to believe in her; he was a little dazzled by her, but, as always, a prey to fretful doubts. In spite of d'Alençon's whole-hearted championship, in spite of the secret sign by which she had proved to him that he was the true King and she the chosen of Heaven, he hesitated.

De Baudricourt had applied the test of exorcism to convince himself: Charles determined likewise to push the responsibility on to the Church. The credit, if any, of her exploits would then be his and, if she failed, no one would be able to blame him. He had often besought Heaven in prayer for a miracle which would save France; now the miracle had been vouchsafed, but it had taken a disconcerting form. He saw himself being dragged from his life of padded ease by this shouting peasant. Yet, not being entirely base, he had an uncomfortable compulsion to obey the resolute creature, who apparently did not know the meaning of fear or embarrassment.

In the meanwhile Orléans was still besieged; since the Battle of the Herrings no further attempt had been made to relieve it from outside. Over the Dauphin's head La Trémoille had been considering plans for retiring still further; retreating to a prepared position, in fact, in the south-eastern corner of France, leaving the country of the Loire to the victorious invader. This tameness was vehemently opposed by the defenders of Orléans. Orléans must stand. An army must somehow be raised, provisioned, financed—they were ready to turn out their own pockets to provide it. Joan would have wholeheartedly agreed had she known; but Joan, by April, was on her way to Poitiers, there to be examined by a committee of learned doctors on the authenticity of her revelations from Heaven.

The proceedings of the Council of Poitiers were lost, or destroyed, unhappily for Joan, as it proved. She answered the learned men's questions crisply, her good manners curbing her impatience. She longed to be up and doing, but since her Voices had prepared her for setbacks of this sort, she tried to accept delay with a good grace. Only when they told her, reasonably enough, that it was impossible to believe in her ability to lead the armies of France without some sign that she was capable of such a task, did Joan flare up: 'In the name of God (*en nom Dieu*, her favourite exclamation) I did not come to Poitiers to give signs! Only let me go to Orléans, and you will see the signs for which I am sent.'

Her four years of communion with her Saints was fresh in her mind; it was impossible that she should not be believed when she spoke of the heavenly fragrance that hung about them, and of their sweet voices. Joan's danger lay in her stubborn conviction that her own inspiration came from God direct. No one had ever been so sure of themselves; no one had any right to be so calmly certain of what the Church looked upon with pursed lips and head-shakings of doubt. The Church was infallible; there was not room in fifteenth-century France for both of them.

Though the learned men of Poitiers were remarkably open-minded and even tolerant in comparison with her later judges, to Joan they seemed wearisomely hard to convince, as they pondered endlessly over question and answer. Her answers came more sharply as the fret for action possessed her.

Their findings, when at last they released her, were cautious. As far as they could tell she was a pious girl, chaste, honest and simple. In view of the great need and danger of the kingdom it might be as well to let her have her head. She had given them a sensible explanation of why she wore page's dress, which they accepted without comment. It was to appear very differently under the grinding pressure of her Trial. The stories that were already beginning to be circulated of marvellous happenings at her birth, they discounted. Joan impatiently brushed these aside; she did not claim sainthood, no one knew better than she her own unworthiness. But God had lain certain definite commands on her. It was her business to see they were carried out. In the end she treated the priests of Poitiers to the rough side of her tongue, which for some reason seems more than anything to have convinced them of her integrity.

At last, she was permitted to leave Poitiers with a good character. She carried away with her a diminished respect for the learned clergy. For the Church of God in the abstract the peasant in her had the deepest veneration, but little but dislike for the practitioners of the religious profession. Joan had childhood memories of mendicant friars whining at her father's door, grumbling at the food set before them, perfunctory in their prayers, and dirty in their habits. From the conversation of her elders she gathered that the monastic foundations were as grasping in the matter of grazing rights and tithes as the feudal landlords, and the Princes of the Church no nicer in their morals than the riff-raff of the Court. From her brief sojourn among the great of the land she had remarked that Bishops, and even Archbishops, were too inclined to secular pastimes and overfond of the pleasures of this world. She had been ready in her innocence to worship the holder with the sacred office he held.

The Dauphin had removed his entourage to Tours, and there poor Joan was to undergo a test of another sort. At Tours the redoubtable Queen Yolande had her Court, and this grave lady, with others of sober reputation, took it upon herself to prove that the miraculous virgin of Domrémy was a virgin indeed. If she were not, then all her protestations of Heavenly inspiration were valueless. If she were, then the Devil could have no part in her.

As in the case of the exorcism by the priest of Vaucouleurs, Joan's feelings were wounded and she wept. Not, as one might have supposed, from embarrassment at having to undergo such an examination and at the hands of a Queen, but at the world's doubting of her. But her common sense, as usual, triumphed. One can picture her drying her tears and squaring her shoulders. Those who go about God's business must take the rough with the smooth!

The ladies were unanimous in finding her 'une vraie et entière pucelle.' From now on none would dare question the title by which she loved to call herself: The Maid of France.

In some ways this period may well have been the happiest time of her life. D'Alençon's friendship had established her popularity at Court, her country table manners were circumspect, and her downright humour never damaging or malicious.

The women saw no cause in her for jealousy; Joan would never give them any.

Picture the peasant child, knowing only a country way of life and the hard yoke of poverty, translated to the company of princes. In her father's house the young Joan would not have dared to raise her voice in the presence of her elders, but crept mouse-like about the tasks her mother set her. She had probably never owned a coin to spend, or any personal property beyond the handspun red dress that was uniformly worn by unmarried girls in those parts. Of the world outside the Meuse valley she could have only the vaguest notion.

She had waved good-bye to her weeping, alarmed parents, in January; it was now April, and in those three months a whole new world had unfolded itself at her feet. In that short space the name of Joan of Domrémy had spread through France. The capitulation of Robert de Baudricourt, her ride to Chinon, her reception by the Court, and the vindication of her character and morals by the learned men of Poitiers and the matrons of Tours, had become already legendary. When she walked through the streets the people brought her their children to kiss.

At Tours she was given a household of her own, such as a commissioned leader of the army was entitled to. She had her pages, Louis de Contes and another, Raymond; her faithful watch-dogs, John of Metz and Bertrand de Poulengy; an

equerry who was to be her aide-de-camp and
tutor in arms, Jean d'Aulon; and a monk of the
order of St. Augustine, called Jean Pasquerel, as
her Confessor. Now at last she could hear Mass
and make confession as often as her heart craved.

She was perpetually in the company of the
Dauphin and her *beau duc* d'Alençon. She was
waited on, praised, adored, and better still,
respected; it was a heady experience for seventeen. We are at liberty to suppose that this
experience, while strengthening her natural self-
reliance, may have made her manners a little
overbearing. From being a mere girl, tricked out
as a boy, she had taken a soldier's rôle upon her,
and a high-ranking Captain's at that. A suit of
armour was fitted for her by the Dauphin's
armourer, modestly free from ornamentation. It
was a simple suit of steel protecting the vital parts
of the body with curved plates, hinged for movement, the joints of the body being clothed in light
steel links that were flexible as silk. Her horse had
its own breastplate and coverings.

She needed now only a banner to carry, and
a sword. A Scot, living in Tours, painted on
stiff, white silk the device she described to him;
Christ bearing the world in His hand, between
two angels kneeling, against a powdering of gold
lilies, with the words *Jhesus Maria* on a scroll.
The smaller pennon which her page or helmet-
bearer would carry depicted the Annunciation.
The standard was a lovely thing as well as a holy

symbol, and Joan childishly loved it. Having no arms to bear, she designed her own personal blazon; a white dove flying on a blue field and bearing in its beak a ribbon with words: *De par le Roy du ciel*.

She must have a sword to defend herself if need be, though she had no intention of actively fighting. Confident as ever, she announced that her Voices had told her where to find one. A messenger was sent off with instructions to look behind the altar of the church at Fierbois, where she had stopped to pray to St. Catherine on her road to Chinon. There they would find a sword buried in the ground. The priest of Fierbois obediently dug behind the altar and, just as she had said, unearthed a sword thick with rust. This was impressive, and was taken to be another proof of the Maid's powers of divination. Thinking a rusty sword was a shabby object to send back to Tours, the priest tried to clean it; at a touch the rust fell from it, and the blade, shining as if it had been forged yesterday, was revealed with five crosses engraved upon it. Reverently, the holy thing was handed to the Dauphin's messenger, in a velvet scabbard presented by the people of Fierbois.[1]

The Maid was now equipped. She, who had come to her King with no other earthly possessions than the hack she rode, the page's dress she wore, and an old ring that had belonged to her mother, had now a stable full of horses for her needs, a suit

[1] *Procés de condamnation et réhabilitation de Jeanne d'Arc*, vol. 1.

of armour that had cost a hundred *livres*, a silk banner, a mystic sword with several handsome scabbards (though characteristically she kept it sheathed in damp-proof leather), and a retinue of pages and esquires.

At Blois, to which the Court moved in mid-April, an army was being equipped for the raising of the siege of Orléans. It must be explained that the expression 'raising a siege' meant the relieving of a besieged city; the breaking of a siege, perhaps expresses it better. To lay siege and to raise a siege were two diametrically opposite manœuvres, easily confounded.

The Dauphin still doubted. He would one day give ear to La Trémoille whose theme was caution and delay, and who advanced all the arguments most likely to appeal to a timid nature; it was folly to waste a mint-new army on a stale cause, since Orléans was as good as lost; money was scarce, why throw it away? The next day would come Joan, and to Charles, who hated draughts, Joan's enthusiasm must have seemed like an open window letting in gusts of raw, cold air.

But she had the bulk of public opinion behind her. She had already gained an extraordinary ascendancy over the troops, with whom she had spent every moment when she was not closeted with the Dauphin, or being taught how to manage her armour and the simpler elements of warfare by Jean d'Aulon. It is one of the most striking tributes to Joan's strong personality that she put the fear of God into those hard-bitten mercenaries.

Never for one instant, from the day that St. Michael appeared to her in the orchard at Domrémy, to the moment when her head fell forward and the smoke hid her last agonies, did Joan forget that she was only the instrument of God. When people tried to idolize her, or accused her of having wished to be so idolized, she grew vehement and angry. She knew her own weaknesses: a rather touching love of bright stuffs and handsome faces, an emotional nature easily moved to tears, a dread of the sight of blood, besides a rough tongue and a quick temper. Later when her personality was being strangled in a net of lies, soldiers who had fought under her banner mocked uneasily, and denied her power. Yet they had been among those who had stopped swearing for her sake, gone to confession, sullenly abstained from looting, which up to now they had looked upon as one of the prerogatives of war, and avoided loose women.

She had no standing with the troops; yet they obeyed her, because she was a born leader. The army was no longer to be a disorganized mass of feudal levies, with no spirit of nationality to weld it into a forcible, striking arm. From now on they were God's soldiers, and dedicated to a holy crusade. She would triumphantly demonstrate to them in her own person that God and His Saints were on the side of France. The terrible English cry of ' *Haro!* ' that had frozen men's blood at Agincourt, at Verneuil, at Rouvray, would be swallowed in the shout from four thousand French throats of '*For God and the Maid!*' They believed her; it was impossible not to.

As the army moved out of Blois on the 27th of April 1429, Joan must have felt the spring breeze loosen the stiff silk folds of her standard, and the blazon '*Jhesus Maria*' spread out above her head, as she rode happily among her companions-in-arms. In front went a body of monks bearing a banner showing Christ crucified. These sang as they went the sweet, mournful *Veni creator spiritus*. In that great company rode the men whose fortunes she was to share; the Marshals of France, Boussac de St. Sévère and Gilles de Rais; the notable Gascon, Etienne de Vignolles, known as La Hire; and her own faithful few, de Poulengy, d'Aulon, John of Metz.

Behind marched the soldiery, shriven that morning, sober and circumspect, very unlike the usual appearance presented by a medieval army, of men dawdling out of step and tagging along a ragged following of prostitutes and loafers. This remarkable procession was wound up by a bleating, lowing herd of sheep and cows and wagon loads of food for the besieged city.

Orléans lay not thirty miles off and, between them, deep and unfordable at that season of the year, ran the river Loire.

Chapter Five

The Relief of Orléans

WHILE at Poitiers, undergoing interrogation, Joan had dictated and dispatched a letter to the English Regent which, in her innocent arrogance, she believed would terrify him into abandoning the siege of Orléans. In this letter she called upon him and his lieutenants, in the name of the King of Heaven, to render up the keys of the cities they had taken or it would be the worse for them. She was prepared to give them a chance to behave well; if Bedford would only see reason and not bring destruction upon himself, the French would show themselves to be chivalrous Christians. The naïve impertinence of this must have exasperated Bedford if the letter ever reached him, just as Joan's honest conviction that she could succeed where he had failed exasperated La Trémoille.

Bedford had been doubtful all along about the Orléans campaign. He was suspicious of Burgundy who showed signs of wanting to make a separate peace; the English Government at home grumbled about the cost of the war, and Salisbury, who had learnt the art of war under Henry V, had died of a wound from a stone splinter early in the siege.

A siege, besides being lengthy and expensive, had a deteriorating effect on an army. When Henry V besieged Rouen, starvation drove the townspeople to surrender, but Orléans still had egress to the outside world and convoys bearing food could not always be intercepted. While the English force was inadequate to encircle the entire city, the inhabitants of Orléans were not likely to starve; their chief inconvenience was the overcrowding of the city by country people who had poured in from sacked and devastated suburbs. There were the usual outbreaks of plague; but the town sternly hushed the panic within its gates.

The long winter of 1428–29 dragged past; from time to time the English pounded the walls with stone cannon balls, which the inhabitants flung back at them. The activities of a Frenchman, a Lorrainer, kept the enemy from becoming careless, for it was his habit to conceal himself behind a broken piece of masonry and take pot shots with remarkable precision and accuracy at the English soldiers going about their duties in the meadows below. It is necessary to keep in mind that medieval warfare was excessively slow and clumsy; the infantry soldier was impeded by a huge wooden shield clamped with iron which each man carried on his back to protect him from stones or boiling grease and tar rained from above. This disinclined the besiegers to attack without certainty of success. On the ground the fighting was a hand-to-hand affair between heavily-encumbered men.

When, at the close of December, the English general, Talbot, was joined by the Earl of Suffolk with two thousand men, the besieged community watched with alarm the building of earthworks and wooden forts to accommodate the besiegers. The spring of 1429 brought no renewal of hope to the weary townspeople, who every day waited for the attack which the English seemed unwilling to make.

It is difficult for us, thinking in terms of the speed of modern warfare, to understand how the English could have taken seven months to entrench themselves on two sides only of the city they were besieging, or to picture the scuffles that took place under the impressive name of '*escarmouches, grandes et terribles*'; when one man would be killed outright, one knocked senseless by a flying stone, and two or three more taken prisoner through tripping up in their heavy accoutrements.

Tremendous respect was paid to the conventions governing medieval warfare. Even the Bastard of Orléans, the city's defender, great and enlightened soldier as he was, was prepared to play the endless game of feints, sorties, and retreats, that wore down the patience alike of besieger and besieged.

Joan, in her invincible ignorance, smashed through all this. Her common sense told her that

97

nothing is so wasteful and disintegrating as failure. Frenchmen needed to prove to themselves that the enemy was not invincible, to explode for ever the legend that the English had only to utter their ominous battle-cry for the walls to crumble. She was not yet a soldier, but she had one high qualification for leadership, the inability to recognize defeat.

There was much thankfulness within the city when the word went round on Friday, April 29th, that an army, many thousands strong, was approaching from the direction of Blois along the far bank of the Loire, and that the Maid herself, rumours of whom had already reached the city, had been seen in white armour riding among a great galaxy of knights.

It was rumoured, also, that along with the relieving force were a number of experienced Captains, among them La Hire, the foulest-mouthed and ablest cavalry soldier in France. His famous prayer is often quoted: 'Sir God, I pray You to do for La Hire that which La Hire would do for You, if You were a captain and La Hire were God.' (It brings to the mind the prayer of another great soldier of our own, Sir Jacob Astley, on the night before Edgehill: 'Lord, I shall be very busy this day. I may forget Thee, but do not Thou forget me.')

This rough Gascon accepted Joan as a friend and equal, perceiving in her something of his own stubborn temper. For her sake he repressed the obscenities that came naturally to his tongue, and adopted her own expression, 'En nom Dieu,' which must have sounded strangely school-girlish on those lips. He liked and admired her, but on this first occasion he lent himself to a bit of trickery which is hard for us to understand. Perhaps he was overruled by others more cautious and less believing.

Joan had not troubled herself to enquire about the route. Their progress was so slow that they slept a night in a field on the way, lying down in all their equipment, the grooms and pages dozing on their feet among the horses, Joan found the weight of her armour painful and sleep impossible; she was not in the sweetest of tempers when their journey brought them in sight of the first of the English fortifications, with the spires of Orléans five miles off, and the river Loire running deep and swift between, and she realized that her Captains did not mean—had never meant—to let her attack.

Her anger was not the pettishness of a conceited girl, but of a leader of men. She knew that the soldiers behind her were in fighting trim, fresh, eager, and unspoiled by failure. It must have dawned on her that La Hire and the rest had all this while regarded her indulgently as a sort of regimental mascot; they did not respect her judgment or trust her inspiration. They were infected with the defeatist point of view, held by the Dauphin and La Trémoille, that a brand-new army was too good to waste. In a mounting fury she turned on them; why had they brought her in this way, by the back door, as it were, when Talbot and his Englishmen lay on the other three sides of the city? The Loire was in flood, and the transporting of an army across it would mean endless delay and be at best a slow and dangerous business.

She was greeted by the Commander of the garrison at Orléans, the Bastard of Orléans himself (brother of the captive Duke, later to be known as the Count Dunois), who had crossed in a small boat with some difficulty as the wind was blowing hard down-stream. It was by now raining steadily. Being a great gentleman and of royal blood, he did not allow himself to be provoked by this rough-tongued country girl, who shouted at him as if he were a careless cowherd. He waited till she had finished, and courteously explained that it had been thought better and wiser to load the supplies of food and cattle which had come with the army from Blois on to barges, and ship them across on this side of the city where the English defences were weakest.

'*En nom Dieu*,' Joan cried out, 'the Lord's counsel is wiser and better than yours. . .!' For how could they doubt that she knew best, she who had received instructions from God and His Saints? Apparently they could doubt it. The Bastard had all the logic on his side; he was, after all, a professional soldier. The need of the people inside the walls was urgent. It would be madness to risk open battle with the English, impeded by baggage wagons and livestock. If only the wind would change to enable the barges to be loaded, the cattle could be driven into the city by the Porte de Bourgoyne, while a small force engaged the English garrison at St. Loup (the only fortification that overlooked that side). Joan herself would then make an entry into the City that waited to welcome her. There was to be no engagement, no scaling of the city walls, no testing of the brand-new army that Joan's faith and fervour had conjured out of reluctant material.

The Bastard was an experienced soldier, and accustomed to assess the striking power of an army; he believed in numbers, and thought—and in this La Hire and the rest supported him—that Joan's men were not sufficient to oppose the terrible English.

Joan thought differently. He had all the reason on his side; Joan, on hers, had only instinct. As was to happen so often, her instinct, whether or not divinely inspired, was right. She knew how quickly inaction would deteriorate her fine new army, and that the English would never fight if they found they could terrorize the French into giving in, by just shouting '*Haro!*' at them. It was her business to provoke them to give battle. Why else was she here, in full armour, with a company of knights and Marshals and priests, if not to do battle? She answered the rhetorical question herself. Through angry tears and the rain running down her face, she said; 'You thought to deceive me, but you have only deceived yourselves. For I bring you more puissant aid than has ever come to any soldier or city, the help of the King of Heaven. . . .'

As they talked, the banners and pennons fluttering above their heads had strained stiffly in the east wind. Joan, mastering her disappointment, told the Bastard that he must believe in her. As she spoke, the wind changed and began to blow warm and strong from the west. From that hour the Bastard, in his own words, 'believed in Joan as I had not before.'

The cattle and provisions were swiftly shipped across under only half-hearted opposition from the English garrison of the tower of St. Loup. The army was to retrace its steps toward Blois, cross the river by a bridge lower down, and return by another route. But Joan, though she was within sight of the goal to which she had looked for years, since the word of the Archangel Michael had come to her in the orchard at Domrémy, obstinately refused to be parted from the men who trusted her and who for her sake had repented and been shriven. It took all the Bastard's powers of persuasion, added to that of her own fellow Captains, La Hire and the rest, to move her.

She yielded, but sent her faithful, trustworthy

d'Aulon and her confessor Pasquerel along with it. She did not, as it proved rightly, trust anyone else to return her men to her in their present state of grace and goodwill.

She slept that night at a nearby village and entered Orléans on April 29th after dark, with only two hundred lances at her back. The people crowded the narrow streets under the overhanging houses and wept for joy, pressing close to her and holding up their children to be touched by her. Her pennant was accidentally set on fire by a torch, and Joan turned and crushed out the flame with her bare hands 'as one might do that had long followed the wars.'

Their simple faith and admiration restored her damaged confidence. She could do nothing amiss. She was their saviour, their miraculous virgin who could cause favourable winds and extinguish fire with her hands. They treasured every detail of her appearance, so that we know exactly how she looked on her white horse, with a little battle-axe in her hand, with her standard of white and blue and gold carried before her.

Her torchlight progress through the crowded city was attended by prayers of thankfulness, until at last they brought her to the house where she was to lodge, and left her to be disarmed by her pages, to eat a little bread dipped in wine and water, and to extend her bruised, tired body in a bed which was shared by the nine-year-old daughter of her host.

The letter which Joan had sent to the enemy from Poitiers had been treated with rudeness and contempt by the English who threatened to burn the herald who had brought it, and promised to do likewise to the Maid if they caught her. Joan sent another, indignantly demanding the herald's release, at which the English rudely recommended her to go back to herd cows. They had already called her a whore and sorceress, and *vachère*, or cowgirl, seems to have been the limit of their powers of insult.

To understand the position of the English at the siege of Orléans, it is necessary to have a picture of the scene. The city itself was one of the best fortified in the kingdom, being enclosed by a wall over thirty feet high and more than the stature of a man in thickness. Out of this wall rose twenty-four great towers, from which the surrounding countryside could be seen for many miles. On its south side ran the Loire, broad and rushy, sprinkled with flat, grassy islands.

Salisbury had possessed himself of a fortress called the Tourelles, which stood on a bridge connecting the south side of the city with its suburbs on the opposite bank. He sacked the suburbs, blew up the bridge, and fortified the Tourelles with a garrison of five hundred men under an English knight, Sir William Glasdale. Soon afterwards Salisbury was killed by a cannon splinter; it was said that his death was a judgment on him for having broken his pledged word to the captive Duke of Orléans not to damage the Duke's property while he was a prisoner of the English Crown. At all events he was killed, and the English lost in him a fine soldier of the old school.

When Talbot took over command in December 1428, he began the work of erecting fortifications. This went on very slowly until the town was irregularly girdled by a string of scattered bastilles or forts, strongest on the west, where there were five close together, weakest on the south and east. The Bastille de St. Loup was an outpost about two miles away up-stream, commanding the road to Blois. It was not very surprising that convoys of provisions had been able to elude the besiegers and get into the city from time to time.

The English appear to have thought that they had all time at their disposal, for the work of building the forts went forward very slowly, possibly on account of the wetness of that winter and spring of 1428–29.

The problem before Joan was how to storm the English out of their defensive positions. It took her nine days, by dint of personal example and inspired disregard of the conventions of medieval warfare.

The soldiers who had been sent back to Blois on the 28th had not reappeared by the 1st of May, which was a Sunday, and the Bastard, urged by Joan, who feared La Trémoille's influence over her King, rode hurriedly off to see what delayed them, leaving the command of the city in the hands of La Hire. Joan spent the day going about among the people, who showed the symptoms of mounting hysteria; she calmed and heartened them with prayer, as was her wont. Monday passed in this way. By Tuesday evening a messenger brought the news that the Dauphin's army was at last on the road. In the early morning of the 4th, before it was light, Joan rode out to meet her men, and peacefully returned with them to breakfast within the city. It is difficult to understand the reluctance of the English to seize this opportunity of destroying the relieving force. It is possible that in the half darkness they over-estimated its size. It is also possible that, for all their bravado, they believed Joan to possess supernatural powers; or that Glasdale, a tough and hardened war veteran, scorned to engage an army led by a woman, and escorted by priests chanting their office.

The two armies were now roughly equal in numbers, but word had come to the Bastard of an English force not a day's march away under Sir John Fastolf, the man who had scored the victory of the Battle of the Herrings at Rouvray. As it happened, the Bastard was misinformed, but the news had the effect of putting the army of Orléans on its mettle. Joan ordered them to let her know as soon as Fastolf's force was sighted.

She was not going to be tricked a second time.

It is eternally to the credit of that great soldier and gentleman, the Bastard Dunois, that he never lost his temper once with Joan, though she hectored, threatened, reproached, and commanded him as if he were a servant. Like his half-brother, the poet Duke of Orléans, or like his witty father whose death at the hands of Burgundy was one of the indirect causes of the present situation, he had all the kingly graces. At the trial for her rehabilitation he wrote movingly of Joan and his belief in her. But for all that he was not able to save her from burning.

Joan had been up most of the night before, praying, and was out and about before dawn. That afternoon she lay down on her hostess's bed to rest and sleep a little. No one told her that her soldiers, tired of inaction, had sallied out to provoke the English garrison of the Bastille de St. Loup, which, it will be remembered, lay some way outside the town, along the river bank; it is another proof that the captains still regarded her as a regimental mascot, and did not take her abilities as a leader seriously. But they reckoned without her Heavenly counsellors.

Joan woke suddenly from sleep, leapt from her bed, and shouted for her pages to arm her; below in the street there were footsteps running by, all in one direction, toward the Porte de Burgoyne by which the army had that morning entered the city. Louis de Contes, in his recollections of the scene, gives us a vivid impression of the way Joan could make herself felt on occasion. Her Voices had spoken to her in sleep, telling her that there was fighting going on and that she was being left out of it. She shouted to him to buckle her armour, and to someone else to fetch her horse, while she cursed them impartially for concealing from her that the blood of France was being spilt. In a moment she was out and into the saddle, had grabbed the standard which Louis passed down to her from a window in the overhanging upper storey, and was off at a gallop in the direction of the fighting.

At the city gate a woeful sight met her. The French had gone out light-heartedly full of confidence, intending impudently to bait the enemy and had been disconcerted by the rain of arrows that poured from the tower of St. Loup, in which the English had entrenched themselves. There was no organization for a serious engagement; these exploits of arms, or *vaillantises*, were in the nature of challenges or provocations in which some shots were fired, a few prisoners taken, and then the parties retired into their strongholds to fight another day. Such was the leisurely nature of a medieval siege.

But Joan, not being a professional soldier, was horrified to see her army stumbling back across the fields in disorder. A wounded man was carried past her, and for a moment she sickened at the sight of blood. But in another moment she was her executive self again, issuing commands in her deep voice, heartening her men till she had them turned about face, and swarming the defences of St. Loup.

It is probable that she had already discussed with the Bastard the feasibility of making such an attack before Fastolf could bring up reinforcements. With St. Loup in their hands, the eastern and southern aspects of the city would be safe from surprise. (Whether the Bastard and his Captains hoped to carry the fort without her interference will never be known.)

Talbot, who had his headquarters in one of the completed forts on the western aspect, realized the hopelessness of going to the aid of the garrison of St. Loup and left them to their fate.

That night the bells of Orléans crashed from every one of its steeples. St. Loup was a smoking ruin, many English soldiers lay dead in the fields, some who thought to escape by disguising themselves as priests were taken prisoner and escorted into the city with yells of derision and triumph. Joan rode about the field with her confessor, comforting the dying. It was her first taste of war and its terrible consequences, and she wept that night.

Next day, being the Feast of the Ascension, she gave orders that there was to be no fighting, and the men obeyed her and went meekly to confession, to purify themselves for the morrow.

A counsel of war was held that day. The Bastard and his Captains must have been struck by Joan's coolness in rallying the disorganized troops. They had for so long had to reckon with mercenary soldiery to whom fighting was not a matter of honour, but of income. Mercenary soldiers did very much as they pleased and resisted all efforts at discipline.

Joan, with her insistence on confession and sober living, had brought a new element into medieval warfare. Fighting, from being a filthy and infamous business, once purged of self-interest, became a holy crusade. The veterans of the French wars—the Marshal Boussac, La Hire with his great oaths, Gilles de Rais of the dyed beard, the old Sire de Gaucourt, Governor of the town, Ambrose de Loré and Poton de Saintrailles, soldiers of fortune, and the rest—were not sure that they did not prefer the old ways.

At all events they met towards the evening of the Feast of the Ascension to debate a plan of attack, and only asked Joan to attend when they had come privately to a decision. But Joan was not hoodwinked. In her downright way she let them know it, striding up and down the room all the while. 'Tell me truly what you have decided,' she cried peremptorily. 'I have known how to keep a greater secret than that.'

On the evidence of Jean Chartier, writing twenty years later, whatever the Bastard and his Captains agreed, Joan would be quite certain to go contrary. Yet they bore her no ill will for it.

Briefly, their plan was to make a feint against the Bastille de St. Laurent which lay the nearest to the river bank, and to take instead the Tourelles, the key to the city. They would engage Talbot's forces and induce Glasdale from the Tourelles to deprive himself of men to go to his commander's aid. Joan dismissed this scheme in her usual high-handed way as too wasteful and inconclusive. These were the lines upon which the siege had been unsuccessfully conducted for the last seven months. If the feint did not succeed they would be no better off. The Tourelles must be stormed and she would do it.

She had by now sent a third letter to the English, threatening if they did not immediately evacuate the forts, 'to make you such a *hahay* that it will live in perpetual memory.' Glasdale's men returned the usual insults; called her the Armagnac's harlot, and other obscenities. Joan wept, and then dried her eyes and begged Heaven to witness that she had done everything possible to save the enemy from the consequences of his own folly.

The account of the events of the next two days are so packed with incident, that it is like watching a film.

If the leaders of the army were doubtful, the townspeople of Orléans were ready to follow Joan anywhere she chose to lead them: and across the river by a pontoon bridge she led them on the evening of Friday the 6th. The English garrison of the little fort of St. Jean le Blanc on the far bank, seeing them coming, hastily retreated toward the important Bastille des Augustins, which was constructed on the ruins of an abbey, and guarded the broken bridge across the Loire that bore the formidable Tourelles.

To see the scene, not as a tracery of black lines on a map, but through the eyes of that English garrison, we must imagine ourselves in a great flat meadow. Before us lies the Loire, coloured by the sunset, about a quarter of a mile wide at this point. To the right lies an island covered with low scrub, dedicated to the city's patron, St. Aignan. It hides from view the place where the river widens to over half a mile in width. Since it is spring the alders by the river bank and the red-stemmed willows on the island are covered with young leaves. Immediately in front lies the keep of the Tourelles with its twin towers and masses of broken masonry, that were once the seven supporting arches of the bridge. The weather vanes on the city's many spires catch the evening sunlight and clearly comes the music of many bells. It stands high, girdled with walls that rise steeply out of the water, seemingly invincible. To the left, lost in the trees, are the rest of the English fortifications. In the river meadows the peasants call in their pigs and geese from grazing, as if there were nothing more important in the world.

The townspeople, full of enthusiasm, disembarked from the boats and ran to storm the walls of the Augustine monastery. But on hearing that the English were coming up on their left (there had been more rumours of Fastolf's relieving force), panicked, and in headlong alarm swarmed back to the river's edge and fought to get into the boats. It is at this moment that Joan emerges as a resourceful soldier. With La Hire at her side she pressed forward through the crowd, calling them to order, crying: '*En nom Dieu, forward, forward boldly!*' The sight of the Maid and La Hire with couched lances halted them. It was now or never, for the sun was sinking, soon it would be too dark to fight. Jean d'Aulon, who had been left with some men to guard the boats, could not forbear to follow where the Maid led. The French turned back, disconcerting the enemy, hacked down and made prisoners some of them while the rest fled to the Tourelles. The Maid's standard was set up on the walls of the Augustine abbey.

It was a triumph of sheer personality. Why the English turned tail is a mystery, unless they had never really believed in the Maid, and were dumbfounded at the sight of her, her white standard streaming against the background of fiery sky and churning water.

Thus, without any real opposition, the French had gained the command of the upper Loire with the Bastille of St. Loup, and the two forts of the

Augustins and St. Jean le Blanc. It can only be explained by the fact that Talbot and Glasdale were hourly expecting Fastolf's reinforcements.

The Maid returned to the city to nurse a wounded foot. In the *mêlée* she had trodden on one of those unpleasant spiked balls called *chausse-trappes* which are strewn about the field to lame horses. She had dined, breaking her rule of fasting on a Friday because, in her common-sense way, she knew that she would need all her strength for the morrow, when a message was brought to her that the Captains of the army thought it inadvisable to follow up the day's successes. There would be no more sorties till reinforcements came from Blois.

It is difficult to imagine that the Bastard or La Hire was responsible for this tame decision. More probably it came from the older men like de Gaucourt. Joan sent back a reply in her most arrogant vein: 'You have been with your council and I have been with mine. Believe me, my council will endure and will be accomplished; yours will come to nothing.'

She retired to bed, requesting her confessor Pasquerel to rouse her early. 'Stay by my side,' she said to him, 'for tomorrow I will have much to do, more than I ever had yet, and the blood will flow from my body, above my breast.'

Though she had this premonition of the wound she was to receive, Joan never for an instant considered avoiding the fight. Yet she later admitted to fearing pain, and we know that the sight of blood sickened her.

That night fires burned across the river where the French kept vigil in the ruin of the Augustins; but Glasdale from the Tourelles, between, as it were, the Devil and the deep, still gave no sign.

Joan was up before it was light; the hurt to her foot had kept her wakeful. She was buckled into her armour—by now she was getting used to it and it bruised her less—and heard Mass. We have from eye-witnesses a clear little picture of her refusing a dish of trout which her host offered her, saying: 'Keep it for supper, and I will bring back a Goddam to share it, and will return by the bridge.' 'Goddam' was the nickname that the French had for the English soldiers who were always consigning their souls to perdition. The bridge, as every one knew, was a ruin; how, then, could it be crossed?

The taking of the Tourelles occupied a whole day. It began badly; Joan had high words with the veteran Governor of the city, de Gaucourt, who tried to prevent the townspeople from streaming out of the gate after her. Her captains were dubious about the whole business, for the Tourelles were garrisoned by 600 picked men. On the city side there was the broken-off bridge and the river flowing swift and deep between. On the south side was an outwork joined to the Tourelles by a drawbridge. The outwork can best be visualized by thinking of something like a seaside pier jutting out from the land, built of stones and mud, with high walls from behind which arrows could be shot. If it was stormed from the land, the defenders could raise the drawbridge and continue the defence from the Tourelles.

The fighting began at seven in the morning. The French crossed the river and from the opposite bank began the systematic assault of the outwork, which was protected by a deep and slippery ditch. At Joan's side were La Hire, Poton de Saintrailles and Florent d'Illiers, her confessor Pasquerel, young Louis de Contes, Jean d'Aulon, who has left us the clearest account of it, and the Bastard himself.

The English and French both possessed guns, but so unwieldy were they that they did not do much more than add the smell of gunpowder and the flare of fuses to the general uproar. The deadliest fighting was all done hand-to-hand with short battle-axes, or by shooting arrows from concealed positions. The battle machines that in Henry V's day had thundered effectively below the walls of Harfleur needed too many men to handle them and too much space to turn in to be effective in such a close-packed struggle. Up the muddy slopes of the *fosse*, clinging for foothold and handhold, the French soldiers dragged their scaling ladders, and were as often flung back by the English on the walls. The courage and hardihood of the French seemed inexhaustible.

Joan was among them, climbing, slipping,

dodging, accepted by the men as an equal and, we cannot doubt it, wildly happy. But about noon her words of the preceding evening came true; an arrow struck her, and penetrating the steel links of mail that covered her, entered her body above the left breast. She was carried out by a watchful knight who saw her stumble, and heard the English howl with delight to see the witch's skill, as they believed, seep from her with her blood. She was borne beyond the range of the fighting and laid on the trampled grass. Some soldiers wanted to cure her with country charms, harmless enough in themselves. But Joan, who never acted out of character in her life except once, rebuked them for superstition. She pulled out the bulky iron-headed arrow, crying all the time with pain, and allowed the place to be dressed with soothing oils. Pasquerel had joined her and now persuaded her to rest. But she was back again in the thick of it all by the late afternoon, and stayed with her men till the sun had dipped.

The men were by now deadly weary, and the pace had slowed; the *fosse* was full of dead and dying. The Bastard ordered the recall to be sounded, that the dead might be taken up and buried, and the army return to Orléans to rest itself. But before the trumpeters could raise their trumpets to their lips, Joan had given an equally authoritative sign that she was to be obeyed. In the Bastard's own account of the affair she begged him to wait; it is more likely that she high-handedly ordered him to. 'Rest a little, and eat and drink,' she shouted cheerfully to the soldiers standing by, and retired herself to a nearby vineyard to pray.

The dreaded darkness was near. Inside the fortifications of the Tourelles the English bound their wounds, and watched the parley below. Across the river, in the city, lights moved upon the walls as the anxious townspeople strained to peer through the gathering dusk.

The Maid's standard was carried by a Basque. All day long it had been wherever the fighting was hottest. The men had almost as much affection and veneration for it as Joan had herself. Jean d'Aulon, narrator of the siege, was an old soldier in experience, and had instilled into Joan what little she knew of the science of fighting. He saw the weariness that had settled on the spirits of the army, far more damaging than physical exhaustion; a retreat now would make it more difficult to renew the struggle later.

According to his own slightly bombastic account, he called to the standard-bearer, and leapt down into the ditch, the Basque following. Joan, seeing her standard borne away from her, dashed after them. She struggled for possession of it and, in doing so, agitated the flag so that the men behind thought she signalled to them, and hurried after her.

Her strong voice dominated the clamour for

a moment: 'Watch!' she cried, 'till the tail of my standard touches the wall!'

In spite of her wound, she hoisted it up and forward. 'See, it touches!' a soldier yelled. 'Then enter,' she told them, 'all is yours!'

The English were apparently mesmerized by this scene. At the sudden onset of Frenchmen scrambling up and over the parapet of the outwork they retreated to the drawbridge that led to the Tourelles and safety.

In the meanwhile the people of Orléans and the troops left behind to protect them had not been idle. For seven months there had been no bridge, but now, miraculously, there was a bridge! A lead gutter had been found long enough to reach part of the way across, and a carpenter called Champeaux fixed up a wooden beam, bought from one Bazin, presumably a vendor of timber, which joined it to the broken arch. Across this incredibly dangerous makeshift, Nicholas de Giresme, Prior of the Knights of Malta, led a string of men-at-arms. Those on the other side of the river could hardly credit what they saw—men in full armour treading the base-less fabric of an invisible bridge (*haute en l'air, sans avoir aucun appuy*).

Thus the Tourelles was cut off on both hands; many of those within were thrown, or fell, into the river, and drowned. The rest surrendered. The English captains, Sir William Glasdale, Sir William de Moleyns, Lord Poynings, finding themselves faced by the enemy on both sides, turned back to the drawbridge, intending to hack their way out on to dry land.

Joan, on the ramparts of the outwork, saw their danger, and cried with all her strength: 'Clasdas! Clasdas!' (No Frenchman could get his tongue round the name Glasdale.)

A fire-boat had been sent out from the city piled with inflammable refuse. It had drifted under the drawbridge, which, being of wood, began to smoulder. As Glasdale and the rest in their heavy armour set foot on it, the charred planks gave way, and flung them to a terrible death between fire and water. 'Render yourself to the King of Heaven,' Joan cried, seeing it was too late to save them. 'You called me harlot, but I have great pity on your souls, and on the souls of your men.'

By now the Tourelles were alight. The French soldiers who had dared the makeshift bridge returned that way, driving prisoners before them, thus fulfilling Joan's prophecy. The churned waters of the Loire, in which so many gallant English had been drowned, were alight with craft bearing torches, rescuing men for ransom. The bells of the city clanged, the crowds that packed the walls burst into the '*Te Deum laudamus.*' Night fell, but the streets were bright with flares and thronged with rejoicing crowds.

Joan returned to her lodging, had her wound seen to, and ate some pieces of bread dipped in wine thinned with water. She cannot have slept much for the pain, or for the pity in her heart for those who had died that day.

When daylight came, and coldly revealed the destruction, it revealed something even more remarkable. The English had not been idle in the darkness. The forts on the western side that had so long threatened the city were empty. The heavy guns that could not be carried away stood silent. But on the fields beyond the English army was drawn up in battle formation.

A challenge was brought to the leaders of the French. Some were for accepting it, others against it. Joan struggled painfully into a light coat of mail and rode out with her captains. Talbot's army appeared formidable drawn in the formation that had proved invincible at Agincourt. She took one look at it and decided against open combat. It was Sunday, a holy day, a day in which one might fight in self-defence if necessary, but for no other reason. By now she was so well established in the good opinions of the Bastard, La Hire, and the rest, that she was permitted to have the last word.

After hearing a Mass said in the open field she announced: 'It is not the Lord's will we should fight them today. You will get them another time,' and with that the soldiers had to be content. The English marched off in the direction of Meung, and La Hire with his cavalry saw them out of sight.

It seems extraordinary to us that a fine soldier like Talbot should have been content to be a spectator to the taking of the Tourelles and to submit his men to sullen withdrawal: we can only imagine that sieges were not his *métier*, and that he meant to save his army to fight an open battle such as the English excelled at. After having freely called her sorceress and harlot, it must have amazed him to see Joan kneeling in prayer, her hands clasped round the standard bearing the words '*Jhesus Maria.*'

The siege of Orléans had been raised. The French people streamed out of the gates and looted the empty forts, gave hysterical thanks to their patron Saints, feasted and sang in the streets all night to celebrate their deliverance, which to this day is remembered and commemorated with flags and holidays.

Joan was their idol, henceforth to be known as the Maid of Orléans. But Joan was not much interested in the people of Orléans, and when they came to her with sores to touch she told them to heal themselves, for they had as much virtue as she had. Her affection and loyalty were for the princely House of Orléans; a piece of purely feudal sentiment.

But time was pressing. Joan impatiently brushed aside the languor that follows physical achievement. Two great tasks called her. First must be the coronation of Charles, for a king uncrowned was neither flesh nor fowl, but a dangling puppet who could be made to dance by whoever held the strings. Charles must be delivered out of the hands of his favourites and made to stand upright on his own weak ankles and knock knees. After the coronation the leaders of the army would be free to turn their attention to Paris, now crawling with Burgundians. This, to Joan, with her capacity for seeing the main outlines of things and ignoring detail, was the prelude to the re-establishment of a united nation. England might pin down Normandy, sway the sullen Bretons, truckle to the greedy Burgundian Duke, monopolize Flemish trade, but while Paris was in the hands of Frenchmen, France was not English.

Chapter Six

The Road to Rheims

WHATEVER the Regent Bedford may have thought of Joan, he was obliged to admit that her presence in Orléans not only discomfited the defenders of the Tourelles, 'but as well withdrew the courage from the remnant in marvellous wise.' To Bedford, Joan was quite simply 'a disciple and limb of the Fiend,' and the fact that she had put a spell on him explained Suffolk's reluctance to engage the armies which she led.

The tension slackens now; part of the French army went off up-stream to harass the town of Jargeau to which Suffolk had retired. The bulk of the feudal companies melted away back to their farms and Joan left Orléans for Tours, where the Dauphin Charles was travelling to meet her.

It will be remembered that Joan's brother commanders had not seen fit to trust her with their intentions on the march from Chinon to Orléans. No one really believed she would be successful in raising the siege; no one, that is, but her most intimate friends, d'Aulon and the page, Louis de Contes, and her confessor Pasquerel. Charles, once she was well out of sight, had fallen back into his old, easy-going ways. To his type of mind a shallow, fretful cynicism was natural. Joan, the shouting peasant, set his teeth on edge and filled him with an uneasy suspicion that he was being made a laughing-stock. Since the Archbishop of Rheims had bestowed an official blessing on her, Joan must be presumed to be from God, and Charles was ready to admit that Joan at a distance was wonderful. But her loving importunity, her glorification of himself into a ruler worthy of the tradition of St. Louis, made him close his eyes wearily and wish that she had never left her father's hearth in Domrémy.

Joan rode out of Orléans through the orchard country of Touraine in the company of the Maréchal Gilles de Rais. No more incongruous pair can ever have ridden knee to knee than the daughter of Jacques d'Arc and the Marshal of France, who years later was to be arraigned for hideous infamy and to die at the hangman's hands in an ecstasy of self-abnegation. De Rais believed in Joan. His affinity for the freakish side of human nature found the spectacle of a girl in man's armour neither as odd or as shocking as did most of her contemporaries. He himself dyed his little pointed beard bright blue; and that was even odder than a shorn head on a peasant lass. Through the blossoming orchards they rode together in amity, till they came to Tours, where Charles met them.

Seeing there was no choice, and not being entirely base and ungrateful, he had heaved himself out of his cushioned ease at Chinon— 'little Chinon clustered under its amber cliff, overhanging the sleepy Vienne'—where he desired nothing better than to live out his life unmolested, and had come to Tours with banners to greet the saviour of Orléans.

Their meeting was formal since it was conducted in public, but in the privacy of the King's apartments Joan flung formality to the winds, and in her most headlong manner, clasping him about the knees, her eager face lifted to his, begged him to hold no more windy, wordy councils of state, but to yield to her anxiety to see him crowned King of all France. He must trust her: her Voices had said to her *'Fille de Dieu, va, va, va. . . .'* Had she not raised the siege of Orléans in a little over a week?

She did not give tongue to the thought that must have clamoured loudest in her mind, that of the year and a little more that her Saints had allotted the days and months were flying past.

Charles still held back, with the voice of La Trémoille always harping on caution and delay in his ears. Orléans was a great victory certainly, but a solitary victory. The Duke of Burgundy must be wooed; it was known that he was out of tune with his English ally and that the rout of Talbot before Orléans had been a sour delight to him. While Joan clung and clamoured at his knees Charles hesitated, and finally compromised. He would graciously consent to be crowned, but first the army must be reinforced, and all the English strongholds along the Loire retaken. No doubt he thought it would take a long time, in spite of proof that the French army, inspired by the Maid, had, at Orléans, broken the siege of half a year in nine days.

The Maid's part in the raising of the siege was constantly depreciated to him by the wily La Trémoille, in spite of the burning testimony of her fellow captains. Historians of our own day have tried to discredit Joan's abilities as a leader by stressing her ignorance of the science of war. Yet if ever there was a natural-born leader of men, Joan was one, and war in the Middle Ages was not such a scientific affair. According to her fellow captains she had what most generals acquired only after a lifetime of command.

'She was most expert in war, as much in carrying the lance as in mustering a force and ordering the ranks, and in laying the guns . . .' Thus d'Alençon who was her chosen intimate. Dunois, who had had to put up with a good deal of abuse from Joan, in his soberer way was no less praising of her endurance in the field, and paid his tribute to the forceful personality that could redeem a victory from the jaws of defeat.

Since Du Guesclin, the French armies had not

felt the force of such a personality. He had infused into the sullen mercenaries a spirit of nationality that had in the end struck the dreaded Black Prince out of France. Joan had revived this unity of purpose. The serene certainty that her Voices would not betray her made her fearless in the field. She announced with her inimitable air of defeating criticism: 'Success is certain; if I were not assured of this from God I would rather herd sheep than put myself in such great jeopardy.'

Joan was now at the high noon of her short April day. Charles' lukewarm sympathy and La Trémoille's sneers could not discourage her. With d'Alençon, her *beau duc*, in charge of all the armies of the Crown, she returned to Orléans in the second week of June (1429), to receive fresh arms, the thank-offering of the liberated town.

From there the re-equipped army of France marched upon Jargeau, where Suffolk was waiting. After an initial setback, due chiefly to the carelessness of the too-young enthusiasts, the town fell to them. Joan's *beau et gentil duc* was perhaps more at home in the management of his hawk and hound. Before Joan's invincible self-confidence he was a straw in the wind; when he would prudently have restrained her she gaily reminded him of a promise she had given earlier in the year to the Duchess, his wife, to bring him safely out of any encounter in which they might be mutually engaged. He could not hold back while she dashed forward, regardless of danger. At the taking of Jargeau a stone struck her and knocked her from the scaling ladder, but she scrambled up and on, crying: 'Up, up, friends! The Lord has judged the English. Take heart, and the place is ours.' She was right. Some psychological unease had begun to undermine the English garrisons; the tide was turning against them, and they saw the mounting confidence of their adversaries like a great wave rolling landward.

It seemed Joan had but to raise her standard so that the sun caught its golden lilies, and the towns in English occupation were hers; thus Beaugency, that fell in a day, and Meung, both lying downstream from Orléans.

At Jargeau, Suffolk was taken prisoner. And from England the captive Duke of Orléans sent letters authorizing the purchase of a suit, in the colours of his house, for the Maid of Orléans to wear. As this suit cost thirteen crowns, which was the price of a good horse, we can imagine Joan prized it.

Talbot, meanwhile, had rashly hurried out of Beaugency, leaving a depleted garrison, in order to urge Fastolf, who was at Joinville, to make a stand. At this rate all Henry V's conquests in Northern France would be lost without the English soldiers having had another chance to terrorize the French by their disciplined solidarity in open combat. This gutter wench whom the French seemed to have been bewitched into following as if she were a shepherdess and they her sheep, would find these English formidable in open battle. Boxed up in the fortifications of Orléans and Jargeau, the English soldiery, those patient stubborn yeomen, had not been able to do themselves justice. Let them but meet the French, pike to pike, in the formation that had proved deadly at Agincourt, at Verneuil, at Rouvray, and then they would see what the witch's spells were worth.

Fastolf, acting on orders from the Regent Bedford, was not so ready to take risks. He moved cautiously, conserving his resources. Unconscious of the fall of Beaugency, he advanced upon the army, coming up with them at evening not far from Meung. The two armies contemplated each other for a little, the usual formal challenge to arms was given by the English herald and refused at Joan's command as the darkness was not far off. 'Tomorrow we shall see you at closer quarters,' she told the messenger. To her fellow captains she had just exclaimed, 'The English are ours! If they hung from the clouds we would yet take them.'

But next day the English were in discreet and orderly retreat in the northward direction of Paris, news having come of the surrender of Beaugency by its hard-pressed garrison.

To d'Alençon's considerable embarrassment,

the army, of which he was nominal leader, was now augmented by the presence of the Constable of France, Arthur of Brittany, Count of Richemont. This unamiable character was La Trémoille's close rival for the King's favours. His mother had married, as her second husband, the English King, Henry IV, and de Richemont took his title from the English town of Richmond. Had he not dreamed of becoming in his western domain as great a power as was his brother-in-law Philip of Burgundy in the east, he might have joined issue with England against the vacillating Dauphin, for he was a fighter by inclination and fought where the odds were biggest.

Curiosity about Joan caused him to plant himself and his men in the path of d'Alençon's advancing forces. D'Alençon, junior in experience to the tough, seasoned soldier, was at a loss to know how to receive him since La Trémoille had strictly charged him to prevent this meeting. But Joan, as usual, overruled him. She was far too sensible to refuse the co-operation of a notable commander, backed by a stout company. She only laughed when de Richemont made the defensive sign of the Cross between them. 'If you come from God I do not fear you,' he announced in his surly fashion, 'for He knows my goodwill; if from the Devil I fear you still less.' Joan was not offended, she was becoming used to this approach, but told him he was welcome. The important business on hand was to drive the English from the Loire; quarrels between princes could be patched up afterwards.

It was at moments like this that Joan's talent for leadership made itself felt. The country of the Beauce in which they found themselves was undulating and, in parts, densely wooded. The French captains were uneasy that Fastolf's legendary forces might be in ambush. At her command the army moved on. 'Ride forward,' she told them. 'We have good guidance.' But it was nervous work, and the other leaders were anxious to keep the Maid, in her too-conspicuous armour and with her white standard, at the back, out of sight for fear of surprise. The slow, nerve-racking advance went on for half a day. Suddenly, near the hamlet of Patay, a stag was startled from its place of hiding and plunged away into the very middle of the English army, which a low thicket of trees hid from view. At once there was a stir and a lot of view-hallooing from the Englishmen, who, equally ignorant of the proximity of the French army, were getting tired of waiting for the attack, and welcomed a diversion. The vanguard of the French, led by La Hire, wheeled and charged upon them with such impetus that, for once, the English bowmen had not time to raise their cross-bows shoulder high.

The rout of Patay—for Fastolf never reached the field, but on hearing of the dismay of his

132

countrymen, made what speed he could to safety and the Regent Bedford—sealed that week of victories. Talbot was taken prisoner and brought before the French captains, d'Alençon, de Richemont, and the Maid. To d'Alençon's: 'Ah, Messire, you did not think this morning that such a thing would befall you?' he replied grimly and shortly: 'It is the fortune of war.'

Talbot may have felt some apprehension at finding himself at such close quarters to the Witch of Lorraine, as if the hot vapours from the regions of the damned must stir about her. But the witch was silent, and her eyes were heavy as if she had been weeping, as indeed she had been; for by the time the rear-guard of the army had reached the field, English dead strewed the turf, the dying still feebly struggled. She had upheld an English 'goddam' in her arms and heard his last confession through a blind rain of tears. Joan could never steel herself to the sight of death.

After Patay, Orléans again. This was the moment when Joan should have insisted on marching to Paris. Soldiers were begging to be allowed to fight for her without pay, the people of Orléans were her slaves, ready to deprive themselves of anything of which their Maid might have need. With the collaboration of Dunois and Arthur of Richemont she might have inspired that daring blow that would have numbed all the English striking power. But her

Saints had not said in so many words: 'Take Paris.' Her sacred mission was to crown her King in his restored city of Rheims. The taking of the French capital would follow logically the crowning of France's King.

She had set her will—and a strong will it had grown to be in the last few months nourished by success and adulation—on seeing Charles crowned. Not till the Primate of France, Regnault de Chartres, Archbishop of Rheims, had anointed the kneeling Dauphin with a particle of that holy oil which St. Rémy had sent in the beak of a dove to the baptism of Clovis, would she rest. Loving bright things, she had set her imagination on a scene of splendour and awe in which she, the village girl of Domrémy, would have a place. It is all of a piece with her pride in her gaudy standard and in her privilege to wear the colours of the princely house of Orléans. She was only seventeen and not yet ready to put away childish things.

Up to now she had achieved triumphantly all that she had set out to achieve; the towns of Burgundian sympathies that lay on the road to Rheims, Auxerre, Troyes, and Chalons, would go down before her as the towns of the Loire had done. She was perfectly confident. She had assured the Archbishop and the Dauphin of it.

Her confidence was contagious. It almost put some stuffing into Charles in spite of La Trémoille's persistent attempts to undermine her influence. For her sake de Richemont swallowed his pride and offered his services to the future King, but not all Joan's pleading could prevail there. The Constable, disgusted, withdrew himself and his men, and Charles, with a half apology, subsided under his favourite's thumb. Not for the first time he reduced Joan to tears by suggesting that it was time she took a holiday.

But these were pin-pricks; outside the Court she was everywhere showered with beatitude. Her lightest words were treasured and interpreted, her garments were believed to carry healing; if she bestowed her name on a child it was sure of benediction, her touch, it was thought, could raise the dead. Joan, in her simple way, was made happy by the warm love of the common people from whom she derived, but when they imputed to her the power to work miracles, she ceased smiling and became uneasy. With her natural good sense she perceived that here was danger, as well as discourtesy to her Saints. She is said to have remarked when reproached for the enthusiasm she caused: 'In truth I do not see how I can keep from it if God does not keep me from it.' But objects of popular veneration have little choice, and she continued to be lauded in spite of the fact that never once in all her career did she attempt to appropriate for herself the credit of a victory. The glory was God's, the labour and sweat were her soldiers'. It was to appear very differently at her Trial, when vanity and hypocrisy were only a few of the accusations brought against her and proved to the satisfaction of her judges.

At the beginning of July the tardy march on Rheims was started. At Auxerre, a town of Burgundian sympathies, the army paused to reprovision and passed peaceably on, La Trémoille being an odd two thousand crowns the richer from a bribe the people of the town had privately offered him to leave them unmolested. At Troyes, after a slight delay, the citizens gave in, partly owing to the influence of a Franciscan friar, a popular preacher, who after some preliminary skirmishing with holy water, pronounced that the Maid was all that she purported to be. At the sight of the Dauphin's following and of the preparation for a siege, which at Joan's suggestion were diplomatically paraded beneath the walls of Troyes, the townspeople judged compromise to be the better part of valour. This was on July 9th. Less than a week later Chalons had meekly followed suit.

At Chalons there were some familiar faces in the crowd; Jacques d'Arc, who had once threatened to drown his daughter if he saw her going off with soldiers, was there, and the labourer Durand Lassois, the least and humblest instrument of God. Others too, from her childhood days in Domrémy, ready to marvel. Joan's two brothers had joined her banner earlier and had witnessed her most spectacular successes. It would be pleasant to linger over this reunion and to imagine the burst of talk and exclamation in the rough country speech she understood best. But already banners were being shaken out in the Cathedral of Rheims, and benches stacked in tiers to accommodate the onlookers.

The people of Rheims were bewildered, but ready for a spectacle. Urged by their Archbishop, who, like so many prelates of the time, had never till now visited his See, but who was anxious that the behaviour of his flock should redound to his credit, and encouraged by the capitulation of Chalons, the City Fathers rendered the keys of the city to the Dauphin on the afternoon of July 16th. The whole army and the Court poured into Rheims on foot and on horseback, and all that night the city hummed with voices and footsteps, and the ringing sound of hammering. Early next morning (it was a Sunday) the Marshals of France, the Lord Admiral and other lords, rode to the nearby Abbey of St. Denis where the holy oil was enshrined, and escorted it to the Cathedral, where the Archbishop was waiting to receive it.

To Joan this relic was of special significance, apart from its awe-inspiring properties, for was not the good St. Rémy the patron saint of the little church at Domrémy where she had often prayed alone, in the awakening consciousness of her great destiny?

The ceremony was long, lasting from nine in the morning till two o'clock in the afternoon. As Regnault the Archbishop in his stiff, gemmed robes raised the crown (a borrowed one lent by the Cathedral Chapter, as the official crown was in enemy hands) over the head of the kneeling Dauphin the crowd raised a great cry of 'Noël!' and there was a fanfare of trumpets that rung and resounded up among the highest galleries.

Joan took her place, without, as far as we know, any demur from those present, beside her King, and all through the long ceremony knelt in her white armour beneath her furled standard. Between her fingers was the standard's shaft, worn smooth with much handling. It was just that it should share the honours since it had borne the struggle.

The eyes of all that uplifted throng were upon the shorn bare head like a boy's, bent in ecstatic prayer. Her emotional nature ennobled for her the pettiness and self-seeking of the actors in this, the greatest scene of her life. This was the moment for which she had been born. . . .

As always at such high moments, she shed tears. When the crowned and anointed Charles VII had repeated the oath of Kingship, she flung herself dramatically on her knees before him, crying: 'My gentle King, now is the will of God fulfilled who decreed that I should bring you to Rheims that you might receive your consecration, to show that you are the true King to whom this realm belongs.' The spontaneous action moved many there to weep. It must have been one of those moments of joy that are very close to heartbreak. It was Joan's last experience of that heady exaltation of which she had drunk deeply in the five months since her setting forth from Domrémy. The heartbreak was all before her.

Chapter Seven

Capture

HISTORY is a slow-grinding mill. Into this mill Joan was now relentlessly drawn, for with all her inherent greatness, as apart from her unique inspiration, she was only incidental to the evolution of the French nation. The wheel had but to revolve once more and the political party for which she fought with such faith and fervour would be ground into oblivion.

With the coronation of her Dauphin, Joan touched her meridian; from now on there could only be a decline. It has been suggested by some of her biographers that from that day—July 17th of the year 1429—her inspiration failed her. She was not again visited by her Voices till they came to tell her of her approaching capture. She had to live and act by the light of her own common sense, her feet tangled in a web of fatuous diplomacy.

The act of coronation could not make a kingly King of Charles. On the very day of his crowning he welcomed an embassy from the Duke of Burgundy which he chose to imagine was sent in good faith, and dallied four days in airy exchange of unsubstantial promises. Burgundy, meanwhile, was swiftly reinforcing Paris with his own followers and a fresh contingent of soldiers that had been sent over from England.

Joan had sent him two letters in her usual hortatory and scriptural vein, to neither of which he replied, exhorting him to make no more war on the holy kingdom of France. But when they told her that he had offered the King of France a fifteen days' truce, she grew doubtful and begged Charles to be wary. The offer was, of course, an impudent mockery. Charles might believe what he chose about his cousin Philip, and La Trémoille accept Burgundian gold to turn a blind eye and a deaf ear to the best interests of his country, but Joan saw quite clearly that Burgundy was not only a bland opportunist but a diplomatic twister, and that the argument of cold steel was the only one he was likely to respect.

In the meanwhile the Regent Bedford was also keyed to a state of irritable tension. He was prepared for the newly-consecrated King to march on Paris. He perceived the fatiguing necessity of getting his small nephew Henry VI over from England to be crowned as a counter-blast to the affair at Rheims. He mistrusted his ally Philip of Burgundy, almost as fervently as did Joan, and news had now come of English garrisons in Normandy having capitulated to the freebooters of the Constable de Richemont. Stories of the magic powers of the French King's

mascot were unnerving his men to the point of
making them desert.

He wrote Charles a letter of challenge,
addressed: 'You that style yourself King,' raking
up the old scandal of the murder of John the
Fearless, Duke of Burgundy, by the Armagnacs
on the bridge of Montereau. He laid strongly to
Charles' account the seduction of ignorant
peasants by such abominable weapons of the
Evil One as disorderly women in men's attire,
and wound up by daring him to open combat.
The tone of the letter, intentionally offensive
and contemptuous, would have goaded most
men to retaliatory action.

Charles, after lingering at Rheims to dally
with the Burgundian envoys, dawdled with his
Court and following along the road that led
southwards, by Château-Thierry. He was thrown
into a familiar state of fretful indecision by
Bedford's letter. He was finding that a conse-
crated King differed from a mere Dauphin
only in that he received a larger share of the
blame when things went wrong. Southward lay
his beloved Touraine, before him was Paris, of
which he had no recollection but unsavoury ones
of his mad father gibbering in a darkened room,
and of the German whore, his mother. Paris
was sprawling with Burgundians, netted with
narrow, stinking alleys, and seething with anti-
Armagnac feeling, while lovely Chinon, where he
longed to be, drowsed on its cliff in the late

summer sunshine. But the Regent's letter could not be ignored, and he allowed himself to be rallied to action by Joan and by the impetuous younger element in the army command.

The two armies met each other not far from Senlis, facing in the direction of Paris. Joan's spirits must have risen momentarily as she saw the French army, *her* army, drawn up in battle formation, but though she spurred forward alone and struck the English palisade with the point of her standard, the enemy seemed unwilling to give battle. As usual the English were relying on the hot-headedness of the French captains, who could never see that particular formation of stolid English pikemen without, as a recent biographer of Joan's has it, 'an irresistible impulse to butt their heads against it.'[1]

There was to be no battle. Bedford had no intention of fighting if it could be avoided; his policy was to embroil yet more deeply the Valois and Burgundian factions by reattributing the murder of Duke John the Fearless to Charles and his Armagnac backers, and having drawn on the French army to within striking distance of Paris, he now prepared to make a bewildering *volte-face*, and leave Burgundy to cope with the city's defence, while he himself withdrew his troops into Normandy, where his brother's conquests were being threatened by the free-lance activities of de Richemont.

[1] *Joan of Arc*, Milton Waldman.

Behind a screen of summer dust the manœuvre was carried out. Though there had been no fighting, the French had an illusion of victory through the immediate capitulation of the town of Senlis, followed by that of Compiègne and Beauvais, who hurried to lay their obedience before the King. Charles was delighted by this bloodless triumph and was gracious to the citizens of Compiègne when they came to him with their keys. He was ready to persuade himself, with La Trémoille's collusion, that Burgundy would negotiate and that Paris would be bought back cheaply. He was not aware that at the very moment when he was exchanging large, empty, smiling promises with the Burgundian ambassadors, Philip of Burgundy was formally renewing his pledge of friendship to England. There had been a time when the rift between the two allies seemed to be widening irretrievably; when a well-devised and disciplined assault by the French on Paris might have carried the day, with the King's army in its first freshness of renewed enthusiasm, and the Maid at its head. But the moment had passed. Charles, with the misplaced deliberation of a self-distrustful temperament, was planning instead a diplomatic *coup*. When Joan came storming to him, demanding that he should bestir himself and take the road to Paris which lay temptingly open, he hid behind La Trémoille's bulk and let that impassive jelly of a man take the impact of the Maid's eloquence. We can imagine, from records left by those who witnessed the scene, that she flung away from that encounter, stung to anger and determined in future to rely only on her own judgment.

By the last week of that August we find her on the high road to St. Denis, that lay five miles out of Paris. Charles had neither given nor withheld consent to this expedition, which it must be admitted had been undertaken in a spirit of bravado rather than of sober judgment.

Joan was growing used to receiving cold looks from the King's entourage, but, since she courted no favours, was not much troubled by them. She knew she could rely on the enthusiasm of her companions-in-arms. There was Guy de Laval, the young Breton, who put his estate in pawn to raise her a following and who has left his ardent testimony to her personality: 'She seemed to me a being altogether divine . . .' and him she could count on, as on her *beau duc* d'Alençon. There were the Maréchaux Gilles de Rais and Boussac de St. Sévère, who had been with her through the epic retaking of Orléans, and her faithful secretary-squire Jean d'Aulon, who never left her. But we do not again hear of Dunois, the Bastard of Orléans, at her side, or of the Gascon La Hire, whom she had taught to invoke his God in more mannerly fashion, and who was now far away in Normandy, having thrown in his lot with de Richemont.

Instead, we have the King's own brother-in-law, Réné of Anjou, Duke of Bar, a character after Joan's own heart, impetuous and gay, who was a link with her first beginnings, for he was son-in-law to that old sick Duke of Lorraine who had given the importunate daughter of Jacques d'Arc a horse. These young men, as Joan afterwards innocently let fall at her trial, were always egging her on, daring her to feats of *vaillantises*, or gallantry, as schoolboys might dare each other to rob an orchard.

Sick of inaction, and mistrustful of Charles' fumbling diplomacy, she cried to d'Alençon, 'By my staff, I wish to see Paris nearer than I have yet seen it. Make ready your men,' and by noon of the 23rd of August she and her *beau duc* were clattering with an escort out of Compiègne *en route* for Senlis where the Count de Vendôme was to join them with a company. Three days later they were at St. Denis and in view of the Capital.

Before Joan left Compiègne, in an absent moment, for her mind was crowded again with the old, happy preoccupations, she sent a careless reply, dictated as she swung herself into the saddle, to a letter from the Count d'Armagnac on the subject of the Papal Schism. It came at an unfortunate moment, and Joan, elated at the prospect of action, took no time to consider her reply. The Count was anxious to have her ruling as to which, in the eyes of God (of whom she was the chosen instrument) of three claimant Popes was the true Pope. Joan can only have had the vaguest idea of Papal politics. But in her high-handed way she sent word to the Count that she would have no answer to give him till Paris was won. Then, when she had a moment to rest, she would consult her Saints in the matter. (It was going to be all too easy for the judges at the trial to prove gross presumption and infringement of the Church's prerogative, against the Maid.)

Charles was extremely glad to see the last of her for the time being. He was busy devising a tortuous piece of diplomacy, and wanted none of her high-handed interference.

Charles was to live to be nicknamed the Well-Served, yet he was a weak and treacherous master. His character has its interesting contradictions. He was not without a dry humour and could see a joke against himself. The portrait that we have of him shows him to have been ugly to the point of grotesqueness, but not vacant or cloddish. There is intelligence in the observant eyes, and a melancholy fatalism in the corners of the mouth. But it was not in him to rise to Joan's high estimation of his character and abilities, though a love affair in later life was for a brief span to transform him into the man of action that Joan tried so hard to see in him.

It is impossible for us to follow the working

147

of Charles' mind at this period. While the Maid
and d'Alençon were at St. Denis, reconnoitring
the defences of Paris, he was at Senlis making
terms with his cousin Burgundy. And such
terms! Inconceivable as it appears to us now,
he was offering Philip an armistice that was to
last till Christmas, and a promise of all the
country that lay on the edge of Burgundian
territory, that is to say, all of Picardy to the sea.
As if this were not enough, the King of France
further gravely handed to his vassal and erst-
while enemy the right to maintain the Burgundian alliance with England, even to the
extent of defending Paris on behalf of the English
against the French. In order to induce Philip
to accept this extraordinary arrangement, he
was prepared to throw in the town of Compiègne
as a 'loan,' or, more plainly, a bribe. But the
town of Compiègne, to its eternal credit, refused
to be party to such a humiliating bargain.

For all its wrongness there was a glimmer of
sense in Charles' reasoning; while the Armagnac
party and the Duke of Burgundy divided the
loyalty of Frenchmen, the English could wreak
havoc at their pleasure. But that does not excuse
his betrayal of Joan's faith in him. There can
be no doubt that he cherished a base hope that
during the attack on Paris the Burgundians would
take her off his hands, and that without her the
younger captains would grow discouraged. He
apparently retained no recollection of the dazzled

148

gratitude he had first felt for the girl from Domrémy; her efforts, not always tactful or well-timed, to stir ambition in him had only thrust him deeper into the sulky apathy that was habitual to him.

Had the Constable de Richemont been still in favour he would never have allowed his King to set the royal seal of France to such a bargain. Not one of the French captains, not Dunois or d'Alençon, or even Gilles de Rais, would have dirtied their hands with it.

In the meanwhile, Joan and her *beau duc* were impatiently awaiting him at St. Denis to the north of Paris. They had satisfied themselves of the best vantage-points for striking at the city, and Joan had dispatched d'Alençon back to Senlis more than once with a peremptory request to the King to delay no longer. If the attack on the Capital had followed hard on the coronation at Rheims, at that crucial moment when the Regent and Duke Philip were out of harmony with each other, it might have carried Charles triumphantly into the hearts of the people of Paris, who had loved his wise grandfather. But the fatal delay had permitted Bedford and Burgundy to patch up their disagreement, to reinforce the garrisons and the outworks of the city, and to spread clever anti-French propaganda. D'Alençon, to please Joan, sent a civil letter from St. Denis to the Provost of Paris, which was returned with insults. Burgundy's police had done their work only too thoroughly; there was not by then a soul in Paris who did not know that the man who called himself King Charles VII of France was probably a bastard, and certainly an Armagnac butcher, with a familiar spirit in the shape of a loose woman ('what she really is God knows. . . .')

It was doomed to failure, though Joan flung all her personality, all her usually contagious self-confidence, into the attack. The contradictory orders that had been issued to the army ever since Rheims, and that had kept it aimlessly on the march backwards and forwards south from Château-Thierry to Provins, then north to Crépy-en-Valois and thence to Compiègne, and now from Senlis to Paris, had taken the edge off its fighting spirit. These contradictory orders were not Joan's. They came from the King. But something was lacking in Joan herself; something that had frozen the mockery of the Dauphin's entourage, that had impressed, in spite of themselves, the doctors of Poitiers, that had carried her across the Loire and upheld her during the storming of the Tourelles, and set her by her King's side in the high moment of the coronation at Rheims.

Not long before, she had been overheard to say that she wished it had pleased God to allow her to lay down her arms and return to mind her father's flocks. This uncharacteristic wish must have been drawn from her by the realization that her peak was reached and left behind. There had been several occasions in the past when Charles had broadly hinted that it was time for her to go home, and Joan had wept indignantly at the suggestion. Was her inspiration failing now, or did some hint of what was coming bewilder and unnerve her? She had been angry at being left out of the war-councils of mature captains before Orléans, protesting that they did not take her mission from God seriously, but only regarded her with indulgence as a freak who might bring them luck. One suspects unhappily that at this stage she had dwindled in the estimation of her colleagues into something little better than a mascot of this sort.

There is some similarity between the attack on Paris and the raising of the siege of Orléans. But at Orléans, Joan's inspirations had been backed by the Bastard and La Hire, for whom even the enthusiastic d'Alençon and the hero-worshipping young Guy de Laval were poor substitutes. The attack on Paris was never seriously contemplated by the King and La Trémoille, who from Senlis held in check the bulk of the army, and Joan's light-hearted companions-in-arms were more interested in showy exploits of *vaillantises* intended to provoke alarm within the walls. The preliminary spying-out of weak places in the enemy's fortifications must have been sketchy. No one apparently realized, till Joan seized a lance from a soldier and tested it, that the water in the second moat immediately below the city walls was too deep to be waded.

Medieval warfare at the best was not scientific. As Andrew Lang puts it: 'By both sides in the struggle there was an exhibition of the absent-minded fashion in which war was understood.' The attack was undertaken in a leisurely manner, not before two in the afternoon, in spite of the Maid's urging. The French army was massed outside the St. Honoré gate that was on the north side of the city's defences and probably the least vulnerable of them all. It was protected by two moats or *fosses*, of which the outer was a deep, wide, grassy ditch between high earth-works. But the water in the inner *fosse*, which had most likely been flooded by the opening of sluice-gates controlled from inside the city, stood higher than a man's head, and no one had apparently given a thought to the provision of light craft or plank bridges. Again to quote Andrew Lang: 'The attack was neither serious nor supported . . . The Maid was alone in her determination to force the fighting. . . .'

The bulk of the French army had strangely, as it seems now, planted itself out of range of the city on a hill called the *Butte des Moulins*, whether against the Maid's wishes or commands we do not know. At any rate the first impetus of attack lacked the determined follow-up that might have carried it over the obstacle of the brimming ditch below, and the Burgundian archers on the walls above. As Joan hesitated, alone, on the high bank of the first moat, looking back to beckon with her standard to those in doubt behind, an arrow entered her thigh between the coat of mail and the thigh piece, knocking her to her knees. She had just called to those up on the walls to surrender the city in the name of Jesus. The answering abuse was swelled with cries of triumph as they saw her stagger and fall.

Fuming, she lay there till night came on, crying to her men to attack and fear nothing, God was on their side. But beyond an exchange of artillery fire and an attempt to bridge the water with faggots, no further attempt was made to storm the defences. Joan was carried from the field at last, the scaling ladders that were to have hoisted Charles' men into his Capital were left strewn about, and the attack was abandoned before it had even been seriously attempted. The summer darkness, under cover of which the walls should have been breached, came down and the firing ceased.

A Burgundian chronicler, who watched the whole abortive action, records: 'The plan of the leaders was rather to injure Paris by a commotion within, than by armed assault. . . .'

Joan had never authoritatively, and with the consent of her heavenly monitors, stated that Paris would be won, but only in her old, impetuous, high-handed way challenged her men to follow her standard and believe in victory. Next morning, in spite of her wound, she rose at dawn and summoned the captains, and urged them eagerly to reopen the assault. By her staff, she swore she would not budge till Paris was captured.

D'Alençon, though aware of La Trémoille's express orders that he was to risk no major engagement, kindled to her enthusiasm, as so often before. He probably guessed how little intention his royal cousin had of fighting for the Capital, but he had a sizable army at his own back and they might yet breach the walls of Paris without drawing on reinforcements. With the Maid at his side d'Alençon was ready to dare anything. But their joyful and hopeful scheming was to be numbed by cold water, poured all unwillingly by emissaries from the King, in the persons of young Clermont and Rénè, Duke of Bar. They had been sent hot-foot, and we may believe it was an uncongenial errand, to command d'Alençon and the Maid to rejoin the King, who had arrived overnight at St. Denis. It was useless to argue and expostulate; the royal decree stood, and sadly the enthusiasts prepared to obey it.

They were not without hope that a lightning blow might yet be struck in a quarter where it was least expected. By order of d'Alençon his sappers had bridged the Seine not far from St. Denis. On the 10th of September, very early in the morning, the army moved off in that direction only to find that the King had himself ordered the destruction of d'Alençon's temporary bridge. It was no use any longer keeping up the farce of pretence; Charles did not value the crown Joan had pressed upon his head, and was now making undignified haste to get back to more comfortable quarters. By the terms of the recent truce, having handed over most of northern France to Burgundy, he had only his territory south of the Loire left to retreat upon.

Joan did not protest, seeing it was useless; being commanded to accompany the King, she left her suit of armour—the livery of her short service-in-arms—in the Cathedral of St. Denis. It was a symbolic act. In that austere and noble church all the Kings of France lay buried, and there, too, was embalmed the heart of Bertrand du Guesclin, *'estoc d'honneur et arbre de vaillance'*— the stem of honour, the valiant tree! The pieces of her armour, unadorned save for the dents received in battle—(*Orléans*, *Jargeau*, *Patay*— already seeming dream-like and far away) she laid before the feet of the Virgin. They were later sold by the Burgundians.

Her Saints had taken pity on her and healed her thigh wound in five days, but they did not bid her to make another attempt on Paris.

At Gien, where the King's household rested, she parted from d'Alençon, who wished to rejoin his wife and see after his estates. Neither of them

155

can have supposed that this was their last fare-well, for how could they know that those who governed the King's uncertain humours *'ne vouldrait oncques consentir, ne faire, ne souffrir, que la Pucelle et le duc d'Alencon fussent ensemble'*? The King's governors had their good reasons; such a league of youth and optimism was quite contrary to their own dreary defeatism.

So Joan's *beau duc* rode away with his follow-ing and thus ended their short but ardent friendship begun at Chinon, where d'Alençon first was astounded by the peasant girl's natural mastery of horsemanship and took upon himself to teach her how to handle a lance as well, on fine spring evenings in the meadows by the river.

Six months had gone by since the Maid's arrival at Chinon, and during that time the obscure daughter of Jacques d'Arc had become a highly-controversial figure; alternatively an object of tender and importunate worship, as to the townspeople of freed Orléans; a leader whose personal example was irresistible; a sor-ceress; and a pawn in the political game as played by princes. Of the 'year and a little more' nine months had still to run out; nine wasted, helpless months, before the stern argument of martyrdom was to seal the controversy.

It is painful to contemplate the Maid, her armour laid aside, trailed ignobly hither and thither among the hangers-on that swarmed in the footsteps of royalty.

Small but significant glimpses of her character show through the observation of casual acquaintances; thus, one Margaret La Touroulde, her hostess while the Court lodged in Bourges in the early autumn of 1429, says of her: 'She was very simple and innocent, knowing almost nothing, except in affairs of war.' How should it be otherwise? She had kept her shrewd native humour and rough tongue through all the shoulder-to-shoulder intimacies of campaigning with dukes and princes, because her unique destiny had fixed her as she was when she left her father's house in Domrémy, eternally naïve and unspoiled. If she had been capable of being influenced by external things, aside from her rather childish fondness for bright clothes, had she caught a gloss from the sophistication of the Court, she would not have been Joan, the simple, strong, and innocent Maid.

During this period of inaction, her spirit must often have drooped, but it was always quickly revived by the prospect of a tussle, as at the taking of a small town higher up the river Loire called St. Pierre le Moustier, which she forced to surrender in October. Jean d'Aulon implored her to retreat and not to risk herself, for her soldiers were half-hearted and she stood all alone, exposed to the fire from the walls. Joan, lifting her helmet so as to see better, looked round and replied calmly: 'I am not alone, with me I see fifty thousand of my own men. . . .' D'Aulon could not himself perceive this heavenly reinforcement, nor could the few scared soldiers lurking near, but her confidence was infectious and soon she had the moat bridged and the walls of St. Pierre le Moustier were scaled.

From St. Pierre she ardently desired to go further and attack the town of La Charité some miles down-stream, but there were the usual difficulties about provisioning and equipping a force for a winter campaign. La Charité was in the hands of Burgundian freebooters, and could probably have been bribed to surrender, if the King and his ministers had been sufficiently interested to raise loans for the purpose. But the weather had turned very cold, and nobody felt much like undertaking the expedition but Joan, whose country blood was whipped by night frosts and buffeting winds.

Though we know so little of Joan's movements during these winter months, it is not difficult to gauge her state of mind. Since Rheims, she must have had a rising sense of impending danger. The expressed and explicit command of God had been to free Orléans and lead the Dauphin to Rheims for his consecration. There it had stopped short. She was from there to step blindly and trustfully off what might prove to be the edge of an abyss. The calm, unflustered common sense she showed, her acceptance of setbacks without petulance, and her steady trust in her Saints are not so remarkable when it is remembered that her upbringing had been sober and pious; but set against the background of inherited blood-feuds, the rich, tumultuous tapestry of the fifteenth century, her grasp of essentials and her unassailable loyalty to her King are miracles in themselves.

Charles' present to her that Christmas—the last but one of her life—was a patent of nobility, by which her family received the right to bear arms with the royal lilies of France in perpetuity, under the name of 'du Lys.' This empty gesture was made by the King with much pomp and many references to 'our dear and celebrated saviour'—empty, because no grants of lands or pension went with it. The family of d'Arc would continue to inhabit the cottage with the trampled earthen floor. Charles had already granted her one plea, that her home villages of Domrémy and Greux should be exempt from taxation for all time; it was an unusual, though not a very striking concession. This freedom persisted as far down as the eighteenth century.

Of her two brothers who had earlier joined her standard we know nothing; whether they kept themselves humbly in the background, or boasted and grew over-communicative round the camp fire, or in the tavern, about the homespun beginnings of the celebrated Maid. One of them was to replace de Baudricourt as Governor of Vaucouleurs, but that is all we know.

Joan was not denied freedom of movement; she could and did come and go as she pleased, provided she did not cross over from pro-French territory into the Burgundian lines. January 1430 found her in loyal Orléans; meanwhile Philip of Burgundy was celebrating his third marriage at Bourges.

Stories of the famous Maid had been carried across the Channel, infecting the English people with something of the panic that she had inspired at the taking of Orléans. So much so, that Bedford had found it difficult to command the replacement of two hundred spearmen and over a thousand bowmen that he needed.

It was decided to crown the child Henry VI, who was not yet seven years old, for King of England he must be before he could receive the crown of France.

In September, about the time when Joan turned her face reluctantly from Paris to follow the King on his self-imposed retreat, Bedford called a conference of the Powers. The English had never been popular in Paris, in spite of all Bedford could do to reform its monetary system, give freedom and encouragement to the silk weavers, and impose a humane discipline in prisons. The Parisians hated the Armagnacs,

160

but had sourer looks for the English. As every week brought news from Normandy of villages occupied and towns capitulating to the French freebooters, Bedford decided that his duty lay westward. Normandy, of all his conquests, had been nearest to his dead brother's heart, and so with many misgivings he handed the Regency over to his brother-in-law, Philip of Burgundy. By October he was ready to leave Paris.

The Duke of Bedford was an unemotional Englishman, with an innate respect for constitutional government and a distrust of Gallic over-statement. That the French puppet-king employed a harlot who was also a sorceress to fight his battles for him, was but one more proof that the French knew how to win wars by trickery. Bedford had been astonished at the turn events had taken, at the tame retreat of the armies of the French Crown, and the puppet-King's apparent anxiety to come to terms with his old enemy. Here was more trickery. It disquieted him as much as for a different reason it disquieted Joan. Had they ever met face to face, without the shadow of witchcraft and the stake between them, they might have discovered many things in common.

So Bedford went to Normandy, and Joan dawdled after the Court, with an occasional refreshing visit to Orléans where there was always a heart-warming welcome awaiting her, and something more substantial in the shape of gifts of wine and poultry for her household.

That year of 1430, Easter fell late in April, and the town of Melun on the Seine, south of Paris, capitulated to the Maid in Easter week. From La Trémoille's castle at Sully, where the King and his entourage were guests at this time, Joan slipped away, heartsick with impatience, as one historian has it, of 'gilded inactivity,' and, without the King's knowledge or sanction, attached herself to a small free-lance band who were roaming about under her old companion of the siege of Orléans, Ambrose de Loré, and one Kennedy, a Scot.

(France at that time was full of such roving soldiers of fortune; the French offered high prices for help from Scotland, and Charles had even gone so far on one occasion as to offer the province of Saintonge to James I in return for the services of 6,000 Scots mercenaries. 'These Scots fought bravely for France, though unsuccessfully at Crevant and Verneuil; but it must be owned they set a sufficient value upon their service.'[1])

They had no army and not much money between them, but they had Joan's revived confidence and a stroke of luck that was as heartening as unexpected. The town of Melun, on hearing, we must suppose, that the Maid had resumed arms and taken to the field again, flung off its thraldom to the Anglo-Burgundian alli-

[1] *Europe During The Middle Ages*, Hallam.

ance, drove out the Burgundian garrison and welcomed in the King's partisans.

It was a high moment; it was the Maid's last. For in the moat ditch from which she was watching the rout of some stray Burgundians by the townspeople, while overhead the church bells celebrated their victory and Christ's Resurrection, Joan became aware of that strange stillness in the midst of tumult that heralded the coming of her Voices. They came, St. Margaret and St. Catherine, this time with a solemn warning and exhortation. Before the feast of St. John she would be taken prisoner, for it was so decreed. She must not be amazed, but submit herself and take all in good part. Twice the Voices repeated with bell-like insistence: 'Be not afraid or astounded, but take all things well, for God is with you. . . .'

Later it seems they spoke to her again, but she was readier for them. Coming upon her in that glow of happy triumph, of renewed confidence, the warning had rendered her speechless. Later she prayed, steadying the clamour of her startled nerves with the reassurance of God's watchful providence, so often and so wonderfully proved on her behalf. She begged only to know the hour of her capture, and, pitifully, that she might be permitted to die in that hour. It must have been hard, with her youthful body unhampered by tangling skirts, and the sweet spring wind stirring her shorn hair, to believe the day

163

would come when she would be no longer free. The feast of St. John was only two short months away.

All through her life we are presented again and again with proofs of Joan's physical courage. But at no moment is she revealed as so touchingly defenceless as by that stiff-lipped, half-involuntary prayer that she might be allowed to die, if God willed it, in the hour of capture.

Without a word of what had passed in the moat of Melun she turned her followers in the direction of Lagny-sur-Marne, a town pro-French in sympathy, and on the way engaged with them in a successful skirmish against a party of Burgundian brigands who had been looting villages in the vicinity. The Captain of the band, one Franquet d'Arras, she relinquished, at their own request, to the people of Senlis, who had an old score to pay off. In the church at Lagny she knelt with other young girls of the district, to send up charitable prayers for a baby that had died in convulsions before it could be baptized.

She walked about the little streets of Lagny with the children of the place clustering at her heels, and rode out into the country to hunt down stray Burgundian brigands. She had picked up a Burgundian sword, and sometimes used the flat of the blade to give the miscreants a whacking. (She had driven loose women from the camps that way.) Her own mystic sword, the sword of Our Lady of Fierbois from this

164

time on was no more seen, and she would never divulge what had become of it.

In the meanwhile, King Henry VI of England, accompanied by a great many English nobles, had crossed the Channel, and was at the English port of Calais.

Bedford was tied by the leg in Normandy where there was a situation needing all his skill and firmness. He had been obliged to bribe Burgundy with territorial concessions, which he was only too well aware was bad policy. The crowning of his small nephew as King of France was one more thankless task to be faced. Now came the news that Burgundy with an army was marching on Compiègne, the proud city that had refused to be bartered at Charles' pleasure. It lay on the banks of the river Oise, north of Paris, between the city and Burgundian territory, and on the main highway from Picardy and the sea, by which supplies, road- and river-borne, travelled. The farcical truce between the King and Burgundy had been allowed to lapse; not even Charles still troubled to pretend belief in Burgundy's good faith. But the news was as disquieting for Bedford as for the French; while Compiègne adhered to its expressed loyalty to the French Crown, the English garrison of Paris could not be provisioned. It was a double betrayal.

La Trémoille drew a large part of his substantial income from taxes levied on the town of

Compiègne, and had made a shrewd appointment of one Guillaume de Flavy to be Captain of the city and protect his interests. It is arguable that de Flavy was not very sympathetic to the Maid; without being pro-Anglo-Burgundian, he was himself young, ambitious, and a professional soldier, and he had never fallen under the spell of her strange personality, which had been known to put sensitive people's teeth on edge, and violently antagonize others not so sensitive. It has been argued that de Flavy deliberately betrayed her, but of this there is no real proof.

Joan's return to Senlis, with Melun to her credit, had reinstated her prestige, and on the word of Burgundy's march she rode at the head of an army to Soissons with Poton de Saintrailles, an old friend of the La Hire breed, meaning to cross the river Aisne at Soissons, and take a bold and daring initiative.

The Duke of Burgundy thought the recovery of Compiègne important enough to leave his new wife and attend in person. He was hammering at the small town of Choisy on the river Aisne, which runs into the Oise at a right angle some two miles above Compiègne, with the intention of encircling his objective.

Joan's plan was to ride swiftly northwards and seize Pont l'Evéque, some fifteen to twenty miles away, where a bridge spanned the Oise and commanded all the river traffic. Meanwhile,

Poton was to fling himself on the besiegers of Choisy, who would find themselves cut off from their source of supply at Pont l'Evéque and seriously embarrassed. It nearly came off. The garrison of Pont l'Evéque was surprised, and before it could send for help the Maid's followers had halved its strength and were miles away, riding hard towards Compiègne. But Choisy, not knowing of the nearness of its deliverers, had surrendered a few hours before Poton, who had lost time making a detour to get there, could reach it, thus spoiling Joan's manœuvre. Not daunted, Joan swung east to return to Soissons. From there she could cross the river and attack the Burgundians from the rear. But the loyalty of the town of Soissons had been undermined by Burgundian bribes, and the captain of the town refused her admittance. The army which she led, an affair of fifteen hundred men or thereabouts, turned sullen at this reverse and began deserting in bands. Poton de Saintrailles departed with them. Joan let them go without protest, though to the renegade captain of Soissons she expressed herself forcibly on the subject of traitors. About two hundred men stayed with her, among them d'Aulon and Pasquerel, her secretary-esquire and father confessor, and one of her brothers. To hearten them she cried out in her old, gay, confident tones: 'Par mon martin, I am now going to visit my good friends in Compiegne.'

It was now May and the nights were shortening. That nocturnal ride through the Forest of Compiègne, with every snapping twig sending signals to an unseen enemy, must have needed steady nerves. Joan had no idea of the hour or place of her capture and only a vague date 'about the feast of John' by which to anticipate it. She had always refused to consider danger till it was forced on her. Her Voices had bade her trust in God and all would be well. She rode forward alone in advance of her men, under the faint starlight, vulnerable from attack from ambush, but unhesitant. Let the hour strike when God willed; she was steeled and ready. The feast of St. John was still a month away; to the eyes of her companions she appeared as serenely confident as of old. They rode into Compiègne, having accomplished a fifteen-mile ride in four hours, as the day broke.

De Flavy, the Governor of Compiègne, was brief with her; the Burgundians not only held the village of Coudun on the north, that of Choisy on the east, Clairoix on the west, but now Venette to the south. Compiégne was thus roughly encircled within a radius of about ten to fifteen miles.

The town rose above the river much like Orléans, girdled with high walls, with, in place of the broken bridge and the isolated mass of the Tourelles, a solid and negotiable bridge leading on to a well-made road. It was too tempting; Joan must see for herself just how the land lay (disregarding de Flavy's discouraging looks). With the loyal town at her back and a few kindred spirits by her side, all would go merrily (as at Orléans, as at Patay, as at Melun . . .).

It was getting toward evening of the 23rd of May when the Maid rode out of Compiègne over the bridge towards a small outpost, the place of encampment of Burgundy's advance guard. Burgundy himself was at Coudun, northwards; a little upstream, at Clairoix, was a strong force under the leadership of John of Luxembourg, a notable fighter, and downstream at Venette was an English detachment.

In the water meadows below the bridge lay the hamlet of Margny where a Burgundian captain, one de Noyelles, had set up a post of observation. His small following had taken off their armour, expecting no more demonstrations from within the city that day, when a subdued clamour announced the letting down of the city's main drawbridge, and on their incredulous sight burst the Maid, conspicuous on a grey horse and in a red velvet tunic blazoned with gold.

The ensuing scrap was, at first, unequal. It should have been childishly easy for the French, who were in a secure position with the bridge behind them and a rearguard of archers on the further bank of the river to cover their retreat, if retreat should become necessary. De Flavy had posted bowmen all along the city walls as an extra precaution.

The scuffle with de Noyelle's men raised the white dust of the road, and shattered the evening stillness. The noise was borne to the ears of John of Luxembourg, who, with a few captains, had chosen this temperate time of day to make a leisurely reconnaissance of the outposts. From a rise of ground he saw the fight, and we may suppose the Maid's pennant must have been clearly discernible.

Joan, with Orléans and the Tourelles in her mind, refused to retire across the bridge before she had dispatched or scattered the outpost at Margny. It was then that John of Luxembourg's men joined the affair. The French had intended an *escarmouche* and found themselves in for a fight, and many who could not find foothold on the bridge scrambled for the boats. Joan called to them in her strong, deep voice, assuring them that the discomfiture of the enemy was in their power, rallying them with encouragement and persuasion. When d'Aulon, in a panic, tried to wrench her horse's head round and force it back on to the bridge, she resisted him. '*Taisez-vous!*' she shouted to those who cried they were outnumbered. Twice, by her persistence and example, she forced the Burgundians back, but all the time their numbers were being fed, as small bands were drawn in from the surrounding country.

The Governor of Compiègne was a realist,

and seeing that this engagement looked like becoming a menace to the city itself, gave the order to raise the drawbridge. Out of the tail of her eye Joan saw the last man scramble across and heard the rumbling of the pulleys as the bridge rose into the air, leaving a yawning gap above the racing water.

It was the hour; retreat was impossible. She was alone, brilliantly conspicuous in her red and gold. Her horse was hustled off the road on to the water-logged grassland, where it floundered and stumbled. She had prayed for death in the hour of capture, but so rich a prize was not to be permitted to escape that way. She was stormed at to yield herself to this one and that one, but she clung to her saddle bow as they clutched at her, and answered them: 'I have sworn and given my faith to Another than you, and I will keep my word.' At last a soldier dragged her down, and she was handed over to a lord called the Bastard of Wandonne, among shouts of cheerful rejoicing from the Burgundians, who were a simple, rough lot, and thought it all as entertaining as a sideshow at a fair.

She was not quite alone; with her were taken prisoner d'Aulon, her brother Pierre, and two or three nameless others who had refused to abandon her till they saw the red cloak torn from her shoulders and knew it was useless to fight longer.

Chapter Eight

Journey's End

FROM the moment when she was pulled from her horse by the red cloak she loved to wear, Joan was doomed. The Captain into whose hands she had fallen, John of Luxembourg, was a greedy opportunist. His master, Burgundy, while bearing the Maid no particular personal ill-will, would shrug aside responsibility. Charles, her debtor, would have neither the means nor the initiative to ransom her, and her partisans were scattered and powerless.

Joan had faced and tricked and outmatched the enemy in the field, but there were enemies more implacable waiting in ambush for her, among men wearing the livery of the dedicated life, whose measure she could not hope to take. All through her Trial she flung back clear, unhesitating answers to the tortuous circumlocution of her inquisitors. We are amazed at the sturdy good sense she showed, while every minute that ticked by brought her nearer to the waiting scaffold. The four months of her trial and inquisition were as high a test of fibre as any human being has ever been called on to endure. With one pitiful lapse, she bore it with

an endurance unfortified by a shred of education
or stoic philosophy.

It is tempting to hurry over the events of the
year, all but six days, that was to bear her
inexorably to the stake at Rouen. When all is
said that can be said—that she was, after all,
only an ignorant peasant; that her prison
quarters were probably not much worse than
those the poor hovel in Domrémy provided, and
that she openly preferred the makeshifts of camp
life to the opulence of Charles' Court; that, in
all probability, she was not sensitive to affronts
to her modesty from the guards set over her,
but treated them as she had treated similar
experimental attentions from gentlemen in the
Dauphin's entourage, with rough badinage—
when all that is said, and it is indisputably true—
it must also be remembered that though her
origin was earthy, her visions were of another
texture.

Just as Charles had been, the learned doctors
who conducted her trial were rasped by her
insistence, ignorant, stubborn, invincible, on the
nature of her inspiration. The memory was as
vividly before her as if seven years had not
elapsed since the apparition of St. Michael in
the orchard. As she spoke of it, nostalgia
strengthened the impression; her faith leaned on
the beauty of her Saints.

Her judges were not corrupt men; but they
were frightened by forces they could not control.

The trial of Joan, that was supposedly non-military and non-political, was tainted, since it was financed by English money. It was not a just trial, since the outcome was a foregone conclusion. All the resources and ramifications of canon law were bent on the effort to wrest evidence of guilt from her own lips. What chance had naïve wit, patience, and honesty against such a machine ? 'She was tried under a system which is now universally held to be barbaric and unjust, but which was in her time, and, for that matter, for centuries afterward, in full operation in every ecclesiastical court . . . She was arrested on suspicion, and throughout a Preparatory Process, as it was called . . . it was the business of the court to devise a convincing case against her. This was built up, as her interrogation proceeded, by a court not averse from accepting as evidence, stories from her native village of innocent rustic dances and games. The judges must not be blamed for this abuse of justice; it had, in every sense, the authority of canon law. In fact, the distinguishing feature of the Trial is the immense weight of authority behind it.'[1]

But if her trial and condemnation was a farce, so much more was to be her rehabilitation some twenty-nine years later, that led to the revocation of her sentence, and threw mud at her judges, declaring them to have been corrupt,

[1] *The Trial of Jeanne d'Arc*, by W. P. Barrett.

174

self-interested, unjust. Deceived in their estimate of her they certainly were; arrogant in their assumption of spirituality superior to her innocent intuition; but not corrupt. There was hardly one among them who did not kindle with zeal to save Joan's soul from the danger, as they conceived it, of hell-fire, before which the bonfire in the market place that waited for her earthly body paled as a flame does in strong sunlight. One or two even urged leniency toward the end of the proceedings, when the long gruelling had reduced her sturdiness to pallor. But even they saw her only as an ignorant instrument of damnation, and thought the sour bread of repentance eaten in prison was a merciful alternative to the harsh correction of the stake.

She was taken prisoner in May 1430, but not delivered to the Inquisition till the following January. Her first captor, John of Luxembourg, accepted ten thousand francs as his gratuity for taking the notorious Maid, and passed her on to the Duke of Burgundy, after she had been a prisoner in his castle of Beaurevoir for four months or so. While at Beaurevoir, where she was well and even affectionately treated by the wife, aunt, and daughter of the lord of the castle, she made a spectacular bid for freedom. She leapt from the top of a tower of sixty feet or so and was picked up for dead. It was a crazy and uncharacteristic thing to do, unless we are to assume that fear and unhappiness had so preyed on her mind that she became reckless beyond reason. Her Voices had told her to trust in God and all would be well. Joan had always trusted in God, but with a reservation in favour of common sense. On the tower of Beaurevoir she seems to have abandoned common sense and let panic rule her. Later, she explained this recklessness by her concern for the plight of Compiègne. She was picked up for dead, but she was not, in fact, hurt at all, beyond being stunned and unable to eat for several days. Her Saints forgave her; St. Catherine appeared to her and absolved her from the sin of too great presumption, and told her that Compiègne would be relieved before Martinmas, which duly happened in October of that year.

All this time Charles had made no move, or none that has found its way into the records. There are reports of vague threats of reprisals to Burgundian prisoners if violence were done to the Maid, but they evidently carried no weight with Burgundy. It was easier to listen to La Trémoille, and believe that Joan had brought her bad luck on herself by being too proud to take advice, and too fond of wearing gaudy clothes. It was easier to do nothing and lie low, than to force the Archbishop of Rheims to invalidate the trial by suspending the officiating clerics. As Primate of France, the Archbishop had it in his power to do this, but he had never loved Joan.

No one, it seemed, had loved Joan but the powerless few like d'Alençon, roaming the country with a band of mercenaries, and soldiers of fortune like La Hire, who called no man master.

The spot upon which Joan had been captured outside the walls of Compiègne lay within the diocese of the Bishop of Beauvais. This cleric, Pierre Cauchon by name, was an ambitious man who had suffered some reverses of fortune by not being always quite quick enough in perceiving which was the winning side. By now he was on the side of the English and had received the bishopric of Beauvais, but was looking covetously toward the Archbishopric of Rouen. He had been a member of the Council in France of the little King Henry VI. When Joan came riding from the south, and the towns on the Loire fell before her, Cauchon began to be afraid he had after all chosen the wrong side. When Beauvais fell to the French, he was forced into ignominious retirement and the meditations of revenge. The See of Rouen appeared to be receding farther than ever from his clutch. When the news streamed across Northern France that the Maid was a prisoner in Burgundian hands, Pierre Cauchon saw his chance. In the blaze of Joan's trial and martyrdom his figure is touched with reflected brilliance; but he was not, for all that, to die an Archbishop.

The Regent Bedford was faced with a problem.

To kill the Maid out of hand, though tempting, would not destroy the legend that had grown up round her; it was politically important from the English standpoint that her claim to divine inspiration should be thoroughly discredited, and by her own countrymen. The charge of heresy was a peculiarly easy and effective method of attacking a political enemy. No accusation was easier to bring, none so difficult to disprove. The double Crown of England and France would sit more securely on his young nephew's head, once the Maid was proved to be an instrument of Satan, and Charles' coronation invalidated. To do this, his overtaxed French dominions would have to bear the huge incidental expenses of a trial, as well as the cost of her ransom from Burgundy.

Not, we believe, altogether willingly, the Duke of Bedford allowed Cauchon to go forward with arrangements for the trial. He insisted on an agreement in writing that the Maid should be kept under English supervision. If found guilty, she would be handed over to public execution as was the usual custom, but if—and here Bedford showed his acumen—the learned doctors defeated their own ends by over-subtlety, and allowed the Maid, whose ready answers were notorious, to kick her feet free of the nets set to catch her, then she was to be handed over to the English just the same. Cauchon, naturally, was not pleased at this cynical proviso, but as he depended on English money to place the Maid in his power, he had no choice.

Cauchon had powerful allies; not only among the English, but among the doctors of theology of the University of Paris, of which he was a graduate. When Joan had led the King's armies to the gates of Paris and sent its citizens scuttling into their hide-outs for fear of her, the University had been faced with the unthinkable humiliation of having to abase itself before an ignorant peasant, a presumptuous slut who couldn't write her own name. The greatness of their relief, when the siege of Paris was called off, was the measure of their stored-up vindictiveness against Joan.

The impressive moral authority of the University was founded on spiritual arrogance. As a collective body it could not err in its judgments; it was the supreme arbiter, not second to Rome. The capture of Joan by the Burgundians had placed within its reach a dear privilege: the power to wreak private spleen in the highest interests of the public.

Pierre Cauchon had acquitted himself with honour, even with brilliance, at the University, and had held the post of Rector at a creditably early age. The logical product of the best education Europe could then provide was a nature and intellect such as his, rigidly disciplined, controlled and calculating. Added to this, in Pierre Cauchon's case, was the poison of personal spite and private ambition. This was the man who announced it to be his intention to save the Maid's soul from damnation, even by way of the fire, if need be. Joan summed him up; she was not impressed by his pontifical airs, and saw the latent gleam of malice in his eye. He might have all the vast weight of the moral authority of the University of Paris behind him, but she told him roundly: 'Bishop, you take too much upon yourself.'

From John of Luxembourg's castle of Beaurevoir, Joan was taken by slow stages to Rouen, where the trial was to take place, its Chapter having granted territory to the Bishop of Beauvais upon which to conduct the proceedings, his own episcopate being temporarily in the hands of the enemy. The journey must have been taken with elaborate secrecy, or surely her friends would have mustered to save Joan. Most probably she travelled in some sort of disguise and passed unnoticed through villages and country towns where the rumour of her true identity would have brought partisans to her aid. The Constable de Richemont's men were roaming all over Normandy; at some time on the journey she must have been very near her friends, though powerless to make herself known. Her itinerary was by way of Crotoy, where the river Somme gains the sea, and from there by boat to St. Valery on the far bank, and so to Dieppe, and thence to Rouen, second city of

France. It would obviously have been preferable to hold the trial in Paris, but that Bedford, distrustful of his French allies, preferred to keep the affair under his own eye. So to the already venerable prison, where Richard Coeur-de-Lion had once been held a prisoner, they brought the Maid before Christmas 1430.

It had taken Cauchon all of the seven months since Joan's capture at Compiègne to put the machinery of retribution into motion. Much against his inclination he had had to bargain for her with her captor John of Luxembourg, who was in a position to ask the exorbitant ransom of £10,000, an unheard-of sum for one who was not royal.

Cauchon, himself, received on his own account, for travelling expenses alone, in the neighbourhood of 800 *livres tournois*. He had earned it during those seven months, for it had been hard work collecting damaging facts about Joan's early life and morals. It was always possible for the Inquisition to falsify rumour and distort evidence under questioning, but in this case there was such strong public feeling in Joan's favour that Cauchon had to tread with extreme wariness. He strengthened his hand by assembling a body of assessors who, for one reason or another, wished to keep on the winning side, and who were bound together by a common loyalty in the University whose stringency had made them the men they were, narrow, intolerant, and remorseless.

Such a man was Jean d'Estivet, the promoter, a former Canon of Beauvais, violently pro-English in sympathy, as it was convenient to be in Rouen at that time. Cauchon was the self-appointed judge; his colleague was the representative in Rouen of the Grand Inquisitor of of France, whom business obliged to be absent—one Lemaistre, a Dominican. This man, it seems, from various indications, was most doubtful and unenthusiastic about accepting the honour delegated to him. He was for the most part silent throughout the trial, except in the inescapable performance of his duty as Vicar to the Grand Inquisitor. We know, from the proceedings of the trial for Joan's rehabilitation, that there were other uneasy souls in that crowd of judges, who in one or two cases had the courage to speak up on the Maid's behalf.

Cauchon's personality overrode all. It was to be his triumph, his work of art, his vindication. Revenge, never more sweet than when long premeditated, was his to take. One by one, through his long, predatory fingers, he gathered up the strings, till he had his sombre puppets in disciplined and orderly array; the promoters and the assessors, the secretaries who were to note down the proceedings, the doctors of theology to expound dogma, the lawyers and their clerks, and the rank and file of priests of varying degree. The titular head of the whole affair was the English King's uncle, Henry Beaufort, Bishop of

Winchester, who had a licence from Rome to style himself Cardinal of England. But it was Cauchon who held the court in submission and alarm under the cold glitter of his all-perceiving eye. Joan was, perhaps, the only person present who was not much in awe of him.

Up to now Joan had been well treated. D'Aulon had been taken prisoner with her, and during the early stages, at least, of her imprisonment he was permitted to wait on her. About now he disappears from the scene; we hear of him borrowing money to ransom himself, but do not hear of him again till the trial for the Rehabilitation of the Maid in 1456, to which he brought his slightly confusing though always loyal testimony. Where he went in the meanwhile, the fussy, talkative, honest little Squire, is irrelevant to this narrative, since satellites shine only with reflected light. But one cannot help wishing to know where he was on that May morning—on the high-road or by a friendly hearth, or in some crowded market place—when news came hot from Rouen that the Maid had been formally declared an enemy of the Church, and perished, a relapsed heretic, in the flames.

It was Christmas-time and cuttingly cold. The cell reserved for Joan was up a few steps and was fairly large, large enough to accommodate some sort of a rough bed and to permit three jailers to sleep, as well as the prisoner. There was a heavy wooden beam with an iron staple to which a chain was attached, and a window that let in sufficient light but did not permit a view of the outside world, such as might have enlivened a prisoner's empty hours. Into this dismal place, at the coldest time of the year, Joan was hustled, and the chain was attached by an iron bracelet to the swift feet that once had carried her so gaily. Had that been all it might have been bearable. But the English were taking no chances. Instead of having women about her, as she was entitled to, five soldiers of the English garrison watched her day and night, two outside the door, and three within. And they were not chosen for kindliness, but were of the most depraved type. She was never free of their jeering inquisitive eyes, or of their foul language, and surreptitious attempts upon her modesty. She might walk the length of her cell, but never see out; lie down on her poor mattress, but seldom sleep; she dared not weep and could pray only in silence. Even the friendly darkness was no friend to her, since only by constant vigilance could she prevent her fiendish guard from attacking her, and she dared sleep only when they were drunk and incapable. Her safeguard against rape was her page's doublet and hose, to which she clung day and night, though the old black suit was worn threadbare at knee and elbow.

Though the trial opened in January, the actual interrogation of Joan could not take place till all the evidence against her had been collected and sifted. While waiting to be called, Joan had a variety of visitors from the outside world, some to threaten and browbeat, others merely to exult over the downfall of the notorious witch of Lorraine. Warwick, Governor of the city under the English occupation, visited her, and the Earl of Stafford, a hot-tempered soldier who drew his dagger against the Maid, so incensed was he to see her sitting there on her pallet bed, chained about the ankles but palely composed, even to declaring that if the English had yet another hundred thousand soldiers it would not win them France.

Whether at Bedford's instigation it is not definitely known, but matrons of the city came to examine her, as once before, to prove beyond question that she was still a virgin. These were the only women beside herself who ever entered that horrible cell. The Duchess of Bedford, Burgundy's sister, sent her a gown to wear, but the tailor who brought it was obliged to take it away again. Joan flatly refused to wear it, and gave him a clout besides, for attempting a familiarity to which he no doubt felt himself entitled, since a female prisoner guarded by soldiers was anybody's game. One hardly dares to imagine Joan's state of mind at this time. The Church, which was to arraign and judge her, had arbitrarily denied her the solace of confession and daily communion with God. No priests visited her but those in the pay of the Inquisition who came at night, disguised, to trap her into self-revelation. The sickening travesty of justice that was the Inquisition had no uglier tool than the *agent provocateur*, who lured the victim into making statements that were then used out of their context as evidence. In this case it was one Loiselleur who visited the prison disguised as a shoemaker, and assuming the accent of Lorraine, for which her heart must have been aching, tried to gain her confidence. But no satisfactory record exists of their conversations, and we do not know if Joan poured out her heart to this seeming friend and countryman, or if she recognized him later in the open court, in the more authentic guise of a Canon of Rouen and Cauchon's intimate.

Joan was not quite friendless; in those dim dawns, when her guards lay snoring, St. Catherine and St. Margaret came to her and stood by her bed with words of comfort. Denied, as she was, the comfort of religious observance, she drew upon the deep reservoir of faith filled long ago during murmurous summer hours at the old Chapel of Notre Dame de Bermont. It sustained and calmed her; meanwhile the Church was preparing the scene for her last encounter with an earthly enemy.

The trial of the Maid opened early on the 21st of February. From the stuffy darkness of her cell Joan was taken to the Chapel Royal where the proceedings were to be held. The morning light must have revealed her as pale from lack of air and exercise, as well as distressingly shabby and thin from poor feeding and imprisonment. It was no very formidable figure that stood before the ranked assessors, but from the pandemonium with which her appearance was greeted she might have been the Devil himself. Cauchon motioned her to be seated, and we can imagine with what an irritable frown quelled the noisy pro-English demonstrators packed at the back of the Chapel. Now that the trial was at last about to begin it must be conducted in all reverence and sobriety, as befitted the occasion, not with howls of objurgation.

From that hour, with intervals of a fortnight or more during which she was unable to move from her bed because of illness, Joan was subjected to a steady battery of question, demand, and insinuation, that in one morning would have broken a less steadfast character. We may interpret her visions according to our own private convictions, but there can be no doubt that they sustained her in a miraculous fashion. Imagine her plight! She was friendless—in spite of her repeated requests that there should be among the assessors some unprejudiced persons to represent her. Prowling the streets of Rouen were Englishmen avid for her blood; it would not be easy for the Court to acquit her even if it desired to do so. But her visions had promised her that if she answered boldly God would sustain her, and secure in this promise she held her head high. With the same good-humoured brusqueness that she had shown her captains before Orléans, she prepared to do battle.

She was not to be browbeaten. When requested to promise on oath to answer all questions put to her, she said reasonably enough: 'I do not know what you wish to examine me on. Perhaps you might ask such things as I could not tell.' Not all their repeated admonishings, in which professional charity scarcely veiled a threat, would move her. At last she agreed to answer as truthfully as she could all questions pertaining to matters of faith, with a reservation that on certain subjects, such as her mystic revelations, she would tell only as much as she thought good. She must have had a fair idea of the charges the court had framed against her, though she was being tried on no specific charge, the policy of the Inquisition being to trap its victims into self-betrayal. From all sides questions were hurled at her, some dangerously misleading, others ludicrously irrelevant. Joan kept her head. When they asked her to repeat the Lord's prayer— it being commonly believed that a witch could not utter the Paternoster without shrivelling up— she politely refused, though she said that if a priest would hear her confession she would very gladly repeat it to him in private.

She was told that she must remain in prison,

since she would not give her word not to attempt
to escape, as she had attempted to do at Beaurevoir. Joan was not abashed. 'It is true I wished,
and still wish, to escape,' she said, 'as is lawful for
any captive or prisoner.' Her guards were then
called in, those ignoble, tainted men, and swore
on the holy Gospel to guard her closely, while she,
watching in disdain, said nothing. The first day
ended inconclusively, and she was marched back
to that hateful cell and the jeering companions
of her long, wakeful nights.

Next day the sitting of the Court took place in
the Robing Room of the Castle, probably because
it was too small to accommodate onlookers, and
an impressive assemblage took their seats on the
benches to left and right of the inquisitorial and
episcopal thrones; present were the Abbots of
Fécamp, Jumièges, and Préaux, the Prior of
Longueville, Canons of the Chapter of Rouen,
many doctors of theology and civil law, and the
Inquisitor's deputy, the unhappy Lemaistre, who
had tried, with every excuse he could muster, to
extricate himself from the uncongenial situation
in which he found himself.

Among the forty-eight assessors assembled was
a knot of men, all brilliant, all notable, who were
Cauchon's chosen assistants; Jean Beaupère,
doctor of theology, Canon of Beauvais, and one-
time Rector of the University of Paris, a man of
infinite resource and subtlety; Jean Massieu,
whose business it was to carry out the orders of

the Court, and to accompany Joan to and from her prison—he was never antagonistic to Joan, and came near to endangering himself on that account; Nicolas Loiselleur, the man who visited Joan in a cobbler's disguise, the *agent provocateur* who was to turn away in tears from the spectacle of her last moments; Nicolas Midi, who delivered her funeral sermon; Pierre Maurice, a young man of great attainments who exhorted her, as it seems to us, with tenderness and real charity, and came nearest to shaking her belief in her own judgment; and Thomas de Courcelles, whose modesty was such that he never lifted his eyes from the ground, and who turned his coat neatly at the trial for the Rehabilitation of the Maid. It was he who prepared the official records of the Trial, taking care (but not quite enough care) to expunge his own name from the proceedings.

These were the men with whose faces, inscrutable or avid, Joan was to become so drearily familiar during the three months of her trial, and with them the cruel face of d'Estivet the accuser, the promoter of accusations against her. Below them, at the clerk's table, sat Manchon and Colles, notaries, who were to take down the proceedings, word for word, whose careful work has outlived them, and hollowed them a niche in history. And high in his handsome chair on the dais, where he could command a view of it all, Pierre Cauchon, representing the boundless powers of the Catholic Church, the University of Paris, and the English treasury.

Jean Beaupère opened the interrogation. From the mildness of his manner and his gentle way of speaking it would have been difficult to infer his reputation as a prosecutor. He must have been conscious of the weaknesses of the case against the Maid; he knew that she had been brought to trial on suspicion, on no more reliable evidence than fragments of hearsay and conjecture, and that the Church had stooped to accept alien and tainted money to buy in its victim. It was his business to lead the girl by persuasion to confound herself out of her own mouth and thus present the Court with a case for trial, and the Church with a clear issue.

As obligingly as possible, Joan proceeded to convict herself. During the interrogations that followed she talked readily of her childhood and upbringing. The assessors were presented with the pretty legends of the Ladies' Tree, on which the children of the surrounding villages hung garlands in honour of Our Lady of Domrémy, and of the ancient *Bois Chenu* where the fairies had their dancing floor, and of the magic spring which healed the sick. She admitted to weaving garlands, but said that, to the best of her recollection, she had never seen fairies in the wood. After her first vision she had taken as little part as possible in games or dancing. She more often sang than danced. A legend had sprung up since she left home, that she had received her first Heavenly visitation at the Fairy Tree; she had heard it from her brother, but there was no truth in it. She had heard also of an old prophecy which said a maid should come out of the wood and work miracles, but she put no faith in that either. Joan's freshness and self-confidence, in spite of her nine months' imprisonment, had not begun to wilt. In that hushed, watchful assembly her deep tones rang out. She, who had led the armies of France in the field, was not to be abashed by a parcel of clerics, whispering and nudging each other, obviously more afraid of her than she was of them. Her Saints, now in daily, even hourly, communication with her, had assured her that she had only to answer boldly and all would be well. Answer boldly, and often shrewdly, she did. Unfortunately, in the eyes of assessors this was but one more evidence of presumption. The Church exacted humility from its children, not the sort of cheerful assurance that had put heart into the Maid's companies before Jargeau and Orléans. When she waved a question aside with a lordly '*Passez outre*' (pass over it), or told one of the notaries who had made a slip that if he were not more careful in future she would pull his ears for him, the jurors pursed their lips. This was not the way of contrition.

Beaupère led her with much gentleness from describing the circumstances of her early life, to the apparition of St. Michael in the orchard. Deeply learned in the vagaries of the human heart, he saw at once she was neither a witch nor a hoaxer. He dismissed in his mind the trumpery business of fairies and wishing wells. The question that was to be the high test was yet to come. No one could assume better a deceptive mildness, but Joan's vigilance was not to be easily lulled. The harmless-seeming enquiry, 'In what form did the angels appear to you?' rang a warning bell. 'There is no reply to that, for I have not had leave to answer,' she said crisply, and on being pressed, 'You will get no further reply today.' Some instinct told her that the question might be a trap, which it was. Visions of heavenly personages might only take an authorized form in order to receive the Church's sanction. (A woman had been burnt in Paris not long before for declaring that God had appeared to her in a red cloak.)

Some deep, instinctive reluctance forbade Joan to describe her Saints. But of the voice that spoke to her, *trés bien et bellement* (well and beautifully) out of a luminous cloud, she said guardedly that it seemed to her a worthy voice, and she believed it was sent from God; when she heard the voice a third time she knew that it was the voice of an angel. St. Margaret and St. Catherine, she admitted, were crowned with rare and precious crowns—'to tell this I have God's permission.'

She was to reveal, under pressure, that their

voices were sweet and low, that they spoke in French and breathed a wonderfully sweet scent on the air. She knew well who they were, since they had graciously revealed themselves to her, and she easily distinguished one from the other. (Heresy! Presumption! The whispers went from mouth to mouth. Only the Church could pronounce what visions were holy. The assessors gave each other meaning looks, and the clerks scribbled busily.)

She answered wistfully when it was suggested that her visions might be deceptions of the imagination: 'I saw them with my bodily eyes as well as I see you; when they left me, I wept; and I fain would have had them take me with them too,' and later: 'I saw them with my two eyes, and I believe it was they I saw as firmly as I believe in the existence of God.' When asked if her Saints hated the English, she replied: 'They love whom Our Lord loves, and hate whom He hates,' and again, when asked if St. Margaret addressed her in English: 'Why should she, when she is not on the English side?'

She could even be cheerfully impertinent; when it was slyly suggested that St. Michael had appeared to her naked, she retorted: 'Why should you think Our Lord cannot afford him clothes?' There were some smiles at this that earned a sharp reproof from the high dais.

The gruelling went on. One by one Beaupère presented, with fatal mildness, the points upon which the Church was desirous of convicting the prisoner. They had to prove her a sorceress, a blasphemer, an invoker of demons, an apostate; profane, sacrilegious, seditious, indecent, immodest, presumptuous, guilty of bloodshed, and a seducer of innocent souls. And so elastic were their premises that if she eluded them on one count they were sure to be able to rope her in on another. She did not make it too easy for them. Her candour and ignorance were disarming; questioned as to whom she believed to be the true Pope, she countered by asking if there were two of them! Beaupère hurried her on to the letter from the Count of Armagnac, enquiring of her which of the three sovereign pontiffs he should obey, to which she had dictated a careless reply when half into the saddle, which her secretary, with mistaken zeal, had amplified on his own account. Copies of the letters were read out in Court, but Joan looked blank. Asked if she professed to know, by the counsel of the King of Kings, what the Count ought to believe in this matter, she answered that she knew nothing about it. As for herself she believed one should obey the Holy Father in Rome; she knew nothing of rival Popes. She was invincibly innocent.

Beaupère was to find that she had a baffling way of putting her interlocutors in the wrong. When he asked her if she considered herself to be in God's grace, she replied simply: 'If I am not, may God put me there; and if I am, may

God so keep me. I should be the saddest creature in the world if I knew I were not in His Grace.' She added sensibly that, if she were in a state of mortal sin, Heavenly visitations would hardly be allowed to come to her. No one in that assembly would have dared to answer that particular question, since a state of grace could be perceptible only to the Giver of all grace. Her clear and candid reply found a mark in the hearts of some of her hearers who were later to testify against her judges at the Trial for the Rehabilitation.

Backwards and sideways the questions dodged and tripped her. Joan often had to take refuge in a flat refusal to answer, or in begging for time to consider, or in pathetically referring them to the findings of the learned and holy men who had judged her at Poitiers. She apparently had not yet grasped the political significance of her trial: 'If you do not believe me, send to Poitiers!' was her cry, again and again, a *cri du cœur* received in silence, since it was well known that the findings of the Council of Poitiers in her favour had been either suppressed or conveniently mislaid by Cauchon's orders.

No episode was too small to be raked up and handed round for her inquisitors to make what they could of it. They had to prove her a sorceress; the childish sports about the Fairy Tree were gone into again at length, and the legend of the white butterflies that clung round her standard as she rode into battle, the suffocated baby at Lagny, whom she had restored to breathing; and the old brass ring of her mother's which she always wore and which was supposed to have magic properties.

They had to prove her indecent and immodest; and since they could not impugn her virginity, they hammered the question of her page's dress and shorn head. She answered them shortly that the dress was a small thing—'nay, the least thing.' She had told them times without number that she had done nothing except at the bidding of her Voices. It was expedient and only plain good sense, when she had to live and sleep among men, to wear the guise of a man. 'Since I wear it by God's command and in His service, I do not think I do wrong; and so soon as it shall please God to command it I will put it off.' She dismissed the fairy legends with contempt, and tossed the white butterflies, and the magic ring, and all the rest of the trumpery after them.

Wearily she countered the accusations that were shouted at her from all sides, as the humbler members of the Court became bold, seeing the prisoner so hard-pressed. She had to beg them to speak one at a time, and often her voice was drowned, till Cauchon's frown quelled the uproar to a murmur.

At each sitting of the Court she had been required to take the oath, as on the first day, and each time she steadily refused. She told them reasonably enough: 'Perhaps I shall not answer you truly in many things that you would ask me, concerning my revelations; for perhaps you would constrain me to tell things that I have sworn not to utter, and so I should be perjured, and you would not want that.' When urged, she lost patience, and said: 'I have sworn enough,' and added that all the clergy of Rouen and Paris could not condemn her for sins she had not committed; wherein she proved her tragic innocence. Once she addressed a forcible reproof to Cauchon in his chair, that many then present were to remember: 'You say you are my judge; take good heed of what you do, because in truth I am sent by God, and you are putting yourself in great peril. . . .'

At the beginning of March she fell ill owing to having eaten bad fish—it was the season of Lent— and in her weakness surrendered herself to death. But she was not to be allowed to escape so easily; the Earl of Warwick sent his own doctor to bleed her to make sure that his expensive prize did not slip through his fingers from natural causes. She recovered quickly—her health had always been magnificent—and was able to receive her inquisitors in her cell by the second week of the month.

The nervous strain of the long interrogation and the closeness of her imprisonment were beginning to tell, but she still firmly refused to take the oath they urged on her. 'The more you constrain me to swear,' she said, 'the longer I shall take to tell you.'

Beaupère had been succeeded by Jean de la Fontaine, who reopened the proceedings by going back over the events of the last year. Many of the questions were monotonous repetitions of what had already been explored *ad nauseam* since the opening of the trial. Obediently she answered seemingly pointless enquiries about the paintings on her standard; about the horse she was riding when the Burgundians took her, about how many horses she possessed, about how much money she had, and so on, until la Fontaine brought out his test question about the sign she had given to Charles at Chinon.

To Beaupère she had been alternately silent and evasive on the subject. La Fontaine was not to be evaded. He was helped by the fact of proximity. In the court-room there had been some distance between her and her inquisitors; but in this small, packed cell they pressed closely in on her, so that she felt cornered, and to placate them abandoned her habit of keeping austerely to the bare facts, or taking refuge in disdainful silence. On the spur of the moment she invented a rigmarole about a tangible sign, a rich and precious crown that an angel had given to the King in full view of the nobles and ecclesiastics of his *entourage*. She was weakening and growing confused, and la Fontaine was quick to perceive and pounce upon his advantage. He soon turned the fable inside out and exposed its weakness, then passed swiftly on to ask what excuse she had to offer for having attempted to attack Paris on the Festival of the Virgin. Joan had no answer to this, nor did she defend herself over the leap from the tower at Beaurevoir, but admitted that she had been wrong to tempt God's providence on that occasion, and that she had confessed her error to her Saints and been forgiven; the hurt she had received in falling had been her penance. But, with a flash of her old spirit, added that she was never a prisoner in any place but she would gladly escape, and if she saw the door open, and her English jailers unable to resist, she would do it again with God's permission. God helped those who helped themselves, as the proverb said.

The questions hurled at her, in their persistence and irrelevance, resemble a swarm of gnats buzzing round her head. Wearily she denied that she had ever fallen into the sin of blasphemy; it was not her custom to swear. Her only expressions were '*En nom Dieu*' and '*Notre Dame*,' and if they had been reported otherwise her hearers had misunderstood. She grew impatient when accused, not for the first time, of having stolen a horse belonging to the Bishop of Senlis, and told them roundly that it was not she who had taken it in the first place, that the horse was worthless, and that the Bishop had been paid for it. These things were trifles, but they served to confuse and distress her. La Fontaine next asked her which she would prefer; to wear a woman's dress and be allowed to attend Mass, or to keep her man's attire and be denied Mass. She weighed it; 'Promise me that I may hear Mass if I wear a woman's dress, and I will answer you.' The promise was given readily, too readily. Joan may have caught a sidelong glance, or the shadow of a smile. 'Give me a dress,' she said, 'such as the daughters of your burgesses wear, and a hood, and I will wear it to go and hear Mass, and then on my return I will put on once again the dress I have.' The answer did not please and the offer was not repeated.

Her page's suit, from having been a useful expedient, had become an article of her faith: possibly she cherished a forlorn hope that her friends would make a *sortie* yet and rescue her, and that she would live to feel a horse under her and her standard in her hand again. It is difficult otherwise to explain her obstinate refusal to compromise in this matter.

The case for the Church was by now nearly complete. So that she might not be in any doubt, la Fontaine explained to her, in terms simple enough for an ignorant peasant to understand, the difference between the Church Triumphant in Heaven, where God sits enthroned with the souls of the saved, and the Church Militant on earth, presided over by the Pope (God's Vicar), the Cardinals and the clergy. 'This Church,' Joan was told, 'in good assembly cannot err and is governed by the Holy Spirit.' She was asked if she would submit herself to its ruling.

'I commit myself to Our Lord, who sent me, to Our Lady, and to all the Blessed Saints of Paradise,' Joan replied firmly, and added that she had always supposed that Our Lord and the Church were all one, and therein they ought not to make difficulties for her. 'Why do you make difficulties when it is all one?' she asked in distress. She had once again, in her simplicity, cut clear through dogma to the heart of truth, and in doing so condemned herself. She would submit herself, she said, only to the judgment of the Church Victorious, the judgment of God and her Saints. There must have been a shudder among her hearers at these words. Did she know what she was saying? Did she not realize that in her ignorance and presumption she was going over the heads of the judges, the prosecutors, and assessors? It could not be tolerated. The whole fabric of the Church, and its very foundations, would be menaced if ignorant persons were allowed to establish direct communion with Heaven in this manner.

La Fontaine asked her, dropping his mildness and sounding ominous, if she realized her danger if she thus persisted in error. She said she would rather die than turn back from what her Lord had commanded her. If she were to be brought to justice she only begged the Lords of the Church to grant her the mercy of a woman's dress to wear at the end. She was facing at last the probability that she would die for her obstinate refusal to compromise or conciliate.

St. Catherine had said, during one of her visitations, that she must take everything peacefully, and have no care for her martyrdom, and that in the end she should come to the Kingdom of Paradise. Pathetically she had tried to convince herself that the 'martyrdom' was her imprisonment: it had been just endurable while she believed that God would work a miracle, if need be, to save her. But if there were greater adversity in store for her she still committed herself to her merciful God. From her Saints' assurance she believed she was certain of salvation. 'That is an answer of very great weight,' la Fontaine had said when he heard this; we can imagine he said it almost pityingly. 'I hold it for a very great treasure,' had been Joan's steady reply.

With a touch of pitiful bravado, since she was helplessly a prisoner, chained to a wooden beam, she declared nothing would induce her to swear not to take up arms again in the accomplishing of God's Will.

The assessors retired to Cauchon's house to confer. The flimsy patchwork of evidence against the Maid that had been so laboriously built up during the last three months could now be compressed into an act of indictment; even then it would be an extremely lengthy document consisting of seventy separate articles. The Court had proved to its own satisfaction that she was equally guilty of sorcery, blasphemy, immodest conduct, bloodshed, and sacrilege; now these minor lapses were all swallowed up in the one far more serious sin of error.

It was now approaching Easter, and Joan, in her distress, longed more than ever to attend Mass and to receive the Sacrament. The lawyers exhorted her, by the goodness and piety which she laid claim to, to wear a dress more fitting to her sex, more seemly and modest in every way than her boyish rags. Joan would not bargain; she replied that she would hear Mass dressed as she was, or not at all, adding, 'that this attire did not burden her soul, and was not against the Church.'

She spent that Palm Sunday in her cell alone, except for her guards, for the assessors were busy elsewhere clearing up the indictment. The first stage of the trial had lasted a month—to Joan it must have seemed more like a year. She had not retreated an inch, and that would be her one consolation. This was only the end of the beginning; the beginning of the end was fixed for the Monday following.

In our sympathy for the Maid, we must not forget that her judges had a point of view that seemed to them perfectly reasonable, though their case against her was threadbare. Apart from the strong political issue of the trial, she was under suspicion of having seduced gullible and foolish persons to follow her to their own detriment, by the use of witchcraft. The minds of fifteenth-century churchmen were obsessed by this fear of witchcraft. The Church Militant figured in their imagination as a lighthouse, standing in a howling desolation of heresy, immorality, bloodshed, and magic. Only by the loyalty and obedience of its members could the outer darkness be irradiated by a steady and consistent beam. They could not afford toleration; for the safety of that bastion of holy enlightenment that was God's Church on earth, Joan had to be proved guilty. Joan herself helped them. By her stubbornness in persisting to wear men's clothes, a thing deeply shocking and reprehensible to the minds of that age, by her uncompromising and unflattering honesty, by her childishly arrogant habit of insisting on her own certainty of salvation, she built up, with her own hands, the fire that consumed her. Worse than all these, she had presumed to have direct communication with the Saints, and to have received through them revelations of God's Will. There lay the unforgivable error. The walls of the bastion trembled before the ignorant peasant who dared to say in speaking of her visions to her priestly examiner; *'All light comes not to you alone. . . .'*

The Law had to find her guilty to satisfy its English backers; the Church had to burn her to stamp out an insidious heresy. Therefore they accepted as serious evidence what seems to us a pitiful pack of nonsense; fairy revels, white butterflies, and the like. While it revolts us, we must remember how they were threatened, how vast and black the Powers of Darkness loomed.

All through Lent Joan had fasted, which must have meant going without the one sparse prison meal. When she appeared before the ranked assessors she was a deplorable object—it was commented on by several—but she still had enough spirit to refuse the services of a counsel from among her inquisitors, who would elucidate to her the seventy articles of the indictment. Her reply was polite but firm: 'First, for admonishing me of my salvation and our faith, I thank you, and also all the company. As for the counsel you offer me, I thank you for that, too; but I have no intention of departing from the counsel of Our Lord.' Her opinion of them was only too evident. As she looked from Beaupère to la Fontaine, from d'Estivet, the promoter, who had collected the evidence and embroidered it, to de Courcelles with his modest air of disclaiming responsibility, she saw nothing to reassure her.

The articles were in themselves remarkable. Joan heard how in her youth she had not been instructed in the belief and principles of faith, but had been 'initiated by certain old women in the use of spells, divinations, and other superstitious arts.' She had frequented, also, a certain fairy tree, mostly at night, sometimes during the day; 'particularly, so as to be alone, at hours when in church the divine office was being celebrated.' When dancing she would hang on the boughs garlands of different herbs and flowers, singing the while verses and invocations, spells and evil arts. 'And the next morning the chaplets of flowers would no longer be found there.'

The fantasy piled up. At the age of fifteen she had become an inmate of a brothel in Neufchâteau, and had summoned a certain youth for breach of promise in Toul, and in pursuit of this case, she went frequently to Toul and spent almost everything she had. This young man, knowing she lived a loose life, refused to wed her, for which reason Joan, out of spite, left the establishment.

With growing wonder Joan heard how she had become the mistress of Robert de Baudricourt, and had boasted she would have three sons, of which the first would be Pope, the second Emperor and the third King. She heard it described, at length, how she had abandoned woman's clothes, and 'had her hair cropped short and round like a young fop's,' and how she had dressed herself in rich and sumptuous habits, precious stuffs and furs. And how it was notorious that when she was captured she was wearing a loose cloak of cloth-of-gold. She heard how she had, 'by consulting demons and employing spells, sent for a certain sword hidden in the Church of St. Catherine of Fierbois, which she had maliciously and deceitfully hid, so that by

misleading princes, nobles, clergy, and common
folk, she might more easily induce them to
believe that it was by revelation that she knew
the sword was there.'

She heard how she had put a spell on her ring
and on her standard, and how, incited by her
temerity and her presumption, she had had the
name '*Jhesus Maria*' blazoned on her letters,
from the tenor of which it was manifest that she had
been deceived by evil spirits. Usurping the office
of angels, she had said and affirmed that she was
sent from God, 'even in things tending openly
to violence, the spilling of human blood, which is
absolutely contrary to holiness, and horrible and
abominable to all pious minds.' (This in spite of
her repeated protestations that she had never
taken life, but had always carried her standard in
battle to avoid having to use her sword. They had
got round it by raking up the affair of the
Burgundian freebooter, Franquet d'Arras, whom
she had handed over to the justices of Senlis,
at their own request, and who had been hanged
by them.)

To sum up with regard to her visions, d'Estivet
had written: 'Consequently we can and must
conclude that these revelations and visions, if
Joan ever had them, proceed rather from evil and
lying spirits than from good; and so they must be
presumed by you, in view especially of the
cruelty, pride, bearing, actions, lies, and contradictions, indicated in the several articles, which

may well be said and held to be lawful and entirely legitimate presumptions.'

His lawful and legitimate presumptions ran to a great many pages, and grew more venomous as they proceeded. He stressed cleverly her preference for the society of men; 'the said Joan unashamedly walked with men, refusing to have the company or care of womenfolk, and wished to employ only men whom she made serve in the private offices of her room, and in her secret affairs, a thing unseen and unheard of in a modest or devout woman.' Stung by the insult, Joan answered indignantly that her government, as a captain in the army, was through men; as for where she lodged and slept at night, she usually had a woman with her; when she was fighting she would lie fully dressed and armed. (She might have added that it was no wish of hers that she should be watched day and night by hostile English jailers.)

It was no good. The voice of de Courcelles swept relentlessly on, and came to the sixty-first article which contained la Fontaine's demand that she should submit herself to the Church Militant and Joan's inconceivably rash reply that it was for God, without an intermediary, to judge her, and she committed herself, her acts and her sayings, to Him and His Saints, and not to the judgment of the Church.

The promoter's embroidery of the barest facts was evidently thought redundant and not in the best of taste by the rest of the assessors; at all events the seventy articles were compressed to twelve, and it seems by a more moderate hand than d'Estivet's. (La Fontaine here drops out of the prosecution; one biographer suggests that he backed out in disgust and fled from Rouen about this time in fear of Cauchon's anger.)

Joan, meanwhile, had become ill again, probably from nervous strain and protracted fasting. She had not often ailed, and it alarmed her so much that she thought herself near dying. When Cauchon visited her she begged: 'If my body dies in prison, I trust you will have it buried in holy ground—' but she was told that if she would not obey the Church she could not expect favours from it. As she lay there she was tirelessly exhorted day and night to take counsel of the Church and to trust in it for the salvation of her soul.

The tone of the daily interrogations in the cell had changed; the mosquito swarm of questions had been replaced by bland exhortation; she was now not so much a witness to her own guilt, as a soul lost in error whom it was the Church's charitable mission to save. They wasted a good deal of breath on her, quoting the Scriptures to prove their points. She, who had been wary as a fencer under cross-examination, was helpless before this eloquence. Asked whether she believed the Holy Word was revealed by God, she who could not read answered feebly: 'You know it well, it is good to know that it was.'

Cauchon's demeanour hid a private uneasiness, of that we must feel sure. He had had the twelve articles of the indictment sent to each member of the Court, and to influential clerics outside, endorsed by himself and his small, chosen band of assessors. The resulting consensus of opinion was not as smoothly unanimous as he had hoped and expected. The letters on the subject make very interesting reading. Many are doubtful, and anxious not to commit themselves; nearly all refer the matter to a higher authority, namely the University of Paris. There is an inclination to disclaim responsibility, to agree with the findings of the Court yet prudently to reserve judgment, in case, after all, the woman should turn out to have been genuinely inspired. And at his back all the time were the English clamouring for him to get on with the business and burn the witch. It is something to Cauchon's credit that he kept his head; he had set the trial in motion, it was to have been the crowning of his life's ambition, he would not now have it spoiled by haste or violence.

Accordingly from Wednesday, April 18th till Wednesday, May 9th, Joan was continuously exhorted. She was shown 'how dangerous a thing it is to believe audaciously that one is fit to receive such apparitions and revelations . . . and from it nothing can ensue but . . . the springing up of new sects and many other ills inclining to the overthrow of the Church and the Catholic

people.' And as steadily, with unfailing polite-
ness, she maintained: 'I believe that the Church
Militant cannot err or fail; but in respect of my
deeds and words I submit them to God who
caused me to do what I have done.'

When Joan could rise from her bed she was sent
for to come to her judges in the Grosse Tour of the
Castle. It was dark down there, in the dungeon
that can be seen to this day, which added to the
horror of the sinister shapes of rack and screw and
pulley. Joan looked from the grim faces of her
assessors to the cruel instruments. Again the articles
of indictment were read over to her, though
she must have been sickeningly familiar with them.
She was not to be shaken even by the prospect of
torture; truly, she said, 'if you were to tear
me limb from limb and separate my soul from
my body, I would not tell you anything more,'
and added with a touch of her old spirit, 'and if
I did say anything, I should afterwards declare
that you had compelled me to say it by force.'
The common sense of it disconcerted them, and
the Court hurriedly decided by vote that it was
neither necessary nor expedient to submit her to
the torture, 'seeing the hardness of her heart.'
There were only three dissentient voices and
Thomas de Courcelles' was one.

The protracted game of cat and mouse was
nearly over. By the 19th of the month of May the
University of Paris had returned its ruling on
the obvious, undeniable guilt of the prisoner, and

the members of the Court, who must by now have
been heartily weary of the whole business,
thankfully agreed to adhere to its judgment.
Some may have been silent, but they went
unobserved in the general hubbub of assent. On
May the 23rd, Joan was taken to a room in the
Castle and there admonished for the last time.
It should not be said, if Cauchon could prevent
it, that she had been condemned without being
offered full opportunity to save her soul. As a
brand plucked from hell-fire she would redound
to his credit, no matter what became of her
earthly body. One of the younger canons of
Rouen, Pierre Maurice, made her a speech,
which was reasonable, friendly, and persuasive.
He had a reputation as a preacher, and something of the man shows in his kindly approach:
'Joan, my very dear friend, it is now time, near the
end of your trial, to think well over all that has
been said. . . . Do not permit yourself to be
separated from our Lord Jesus Christ who
created you to be a partaker of His glory. . . .'

The gentleness of his address, after the threats of
torture and the endless sermonizing she had had to
endure, unnerved her. He spoke so winningly
and in such simple words. Of her Voices he told
her: 'You have believed in these apparitions
lightly, instead of turning to God, in devout
prayer, to grant you certainty; and you have not
consulted learned ecclesiastics to enlighten yourself; although considering your condition and

213

the simplicity of your knowledge, you ought to have done so. Take this example: suppose your King had appointed you to defend a fortress, forbidding you to let anyone enter. Would you not refuse to admit whoever claimed to come in his name but brought no letters or authentic sign? Likewise our Lord Jesus Christ, when He ascended into Heaven, committed the government of His Church to the Apostle St. Peter and his successors, forbidding them to receive in the future those who claimed to come in His name, but brought no other token than their own words. . . . First, Joan, you should consider this; if, when you were in your King's domain, a soldier or other person born in his realm had arisen and said, "I will not obey the King or submit to any of his officers," would you not have said, "This man should be condemned"? What shall you say of yourself, who, brought up in the faith of Christ by the sacrament of baptism, have become the daughter of the Church, if you do not obey Christ's officers, that is to say the prelates of the Church?'

It shook her; the soldierly parallel was terribly convincing. Could she have been misled? But she rallied her beliefs, and answered him that if she were condemned and saw the fire and the faggots waiting and the executioner ready to kindle them, she would say nothing else, and would maintain until the end what she had said at her trial. (The clerk who took it down scribbled

the comment *Responsio superba* beside the answer
for posterity to read.)

There was no more to say; she had been
exhorted and was stubborn. It only remained to
pronounce sentence. She was left alone that
night, alone except for her jailers, those hardened
and brutalized men. For four months she had
seen nothing but the four walls of her cell. The
short walk to the court room led past the open door
of a chapel before which she had been glad to
pause daily and make a reverence, till Cauchon
put a stop to it; this and the court room itself
and the other apartments used at various stages
of her interrogation had been all her world.
Out of this dim seclusion into the May sunshine
she was led, early in the morning of the 24th, to
the Abbey of St. Ouen. The walk through the
streets, where the people were going calmly about
their daily business, must have been strange to
her, going to sentence of death. For four months
she had heard nothing of the outside world, had
seen only the clouds and stars passing across the
square of window in her cell. The sun on her
doomed head, the morning smell of new bread,
must have been intolerably poignant at such
a moment.

Against the wall of the Abbey Church of St.
Ouen was an enclosed space. In the middle of
this stood the stake, a tall post with chains,
and on either side were platforms with thrones
for the judges.

Joan was conducted to a stool on one of these, and from it could examine in all its detail the waiting scaffold piled about with small faggots and brushwood. The Cardinal of England, Henry Beaufort, was present and the Lord Bishops of Beauvais and Thérouanne, of Noyon and Norwich; the Abbots of Fécamp, of Rouen, of Jumièges, of Préaux; the Priors of Longueville and St. Lo, and among the many masters of theology and doctors of canon law, her old acquaintances, Jean Beaupère, Pierre Maurice, Nicolas Loiselleur, and Thomas de Courcelles.

It was a brilliant assembly. Guillaume Erard, one of the Canons of Rouen, delivered the oration from the text: 'The branch cannot bear fruit of itself, except it abide in the vine,' among murmurs of approval from the crowd who filled and overflowed the cloisters. Carried away by his own eloquence he declaimed: 'Ah, France, how you have been abused! And Charles, who calls himself your King and ruler, has approved of the deeds of this infamous woman, herself a heretic and schismatic as he is himself.' He repeated this several times till Joan could not stand it any longer, and shouted back: 'By my faith I dare to swear on my life that my King is the most noble Christian of you all. If there is any fault in anything I have done, I charge neither him nor anyone else, for the fault is mine alone.' Loyal to the end, she drew round her own shoulders the mantle of Charles' guilt and cowardice.

At the end of his exhortation Erard asked her whether she would revoke all her words and deeds against the Church. She countered by saying that she referred herself to the Pope. But it was too late for such an appeal. She was told that the Pope was too far away and the judges here assembled were competent to answer for him.

The English soldiers and the crowd were getting restless. Cauchon rose to his feet and began to read the sentence of excommunication. He was half-way through when Joan interrupted him. She did not speak, but made an involuntary gesture as if to arrest the terrible flow of words: '*excommunicate . . . heretical . . . a limb of Satan severed from the Church. . . .*' Erard immediately twitched out of his sleeve a paper containing the previously-prepared act of abjuration and read it over to her in a low voice. She was seen to glance round, at the grave faces of Erard and Loiselleur, at the kindly face of Pierre Maurice, at the bafflement of the crowd and the scowling English soldiers. A quill was pushed into her fingers, and Massieu took her hand and guided her to write the word 'Jehane,' and to put a cross after the name. She smiled up at him. One witness heard her say: 'You take great trouble to convert me,' and: 'I would rather sign than be burned.'

Erard passed the recantation to Cauchon who read it aloud. Immediately there was an uproar. The crowd, done out of a spectacle, tried to push past the soldiers. An English cleric shook his fist in Cauchon's face and loudly accused him of favouring the Maid. Cauchon turned on him. He had stood a good deal of browbeating from his masters, to say nothing of the long strain of the trial. With cold fury he spat at the man: 'In such a cause as this I favour no one. It is my office to seek her salvation rather than her death.'

In spite of this, urged by the growing unrest among the English, Cauchon ordered her to be taken back to the cell she had left that morning, not, as she had the right to expect, to a prison for women only. One of the assessors is reputed to have said to Warwick, who raged that the Maid would escape them yet: 'Do not disturb yourself, my Lord. We shall soon have her again.' The story is open to doubt, but true in essence. There was no way out for Joan. It seemed there was no one she could trust. Her Voices, who had promised that if she answered boldly all would be well with her, had allowed her to come to this pass. Her King had not lifted a finger to save her, she strained her ears in vain for the beat of galloping hoofs which would herald d'Alençon and La Hire. She had been betrayed and abandoned, and the Church for which she had abjured her beloved Saints had deceived and mocked her by flinging her back into the foul cell and among the companions she loathed and feared. With bitterest tears she put on the long dress they brought her and allowed her hair to be shaved.

To her came the Inquisitor's deputy Lemaistre, Nicolas Midi, Loiselleur and de Courcelles, and a young priest, Ysambard de la Pierre. They exhorted her all over again, and promised her a future of 'perpetual imprisonment with the bread of sorrow and the water of affliction, that you may weep for your faults. . . .' Through tears she agreed in all things to obey and submit herself to the Church, and thus they left her.

Their promises were valueless. She had got to die to implement Cauchon's private understanding with the English Regent. If not on the charge of heresy, then on some other; it didn't matter to Bedford, as long as she was publicly disgraced with the Church's approval.

The happenings of the next four days are vouched for by contradictory testimonies produced at the trial for the Rehabilitation; Massieu, the church's officer whose business it was to conduct the prisoner to and from her cell, had evidently established, in private, a sympathetic relationship with her, though he was Cauchon's underling and obliged to subscribe to the findings of his betters. He was not, at all events, an unkind man, and had got into trouble earlier for showing the prisoner too much consideration. To him she told the ugly tale of repeated attempts upon her virtue by her jailers and by an unnamed English Lord, till she was obliged to reassume her page's dress in self-defence. Ysambard de la Pierre told how he had been much moved by the sight of her poor face, disfigured with tears. Another young priest, Martin Ladvenu, was distressed by her plight; she spoke quite freely to these three men, and theirs were the last compassionate faces she saw before the smoke closed round her.

She told Ladvenu that her Voices had spoken to her again when the bells of the churches of Rouen were ringing at the hour of Compline, and in the early morning, and with them a multitude of the Heavenly Host had filled the cell; in her beaten and distressed state she did not know at first whether to receive them as good or evil spirits. She admitted to Ladvenu that the story of the King's 'sign' was fictitious; there had been no sign, only her promise to him that she would have him crowned at Rheims if he would but trust her.

Human memory being fallible, the depositions of these men are unreliable. Massieu's story is the most circumstantial. Her page's suit, after she had taken it off, was handed over to the English guards. She woke on the Sunday morning, after three days of wearing female garments, and asked for her woman's dress in order that she might leave the cell. Her legs were again chained to a wooden beam, and the chains padlocked. Her jailers refused to unlock her, but on her repeated requests threw the old, black doublet and hose on the bed and told her that if she wanted to get up she must put them on. She protested and implored, till nature would no longer be denied, and she had to agree. On returning to the cell she found the dress had disappeared. The story sounds convincing, but as Andrew Lang remarks: 'Massieu was a man of loose life, perhaps of loose tongue.'

Whatever the reason, there she was, once more in men's clothing, and therefore in a state of relapse. It was what Cauchon had been waiting for, perhaps he had even planned it. Rouen was meanwhile in an uproar. The English Governors were angry, the soldiers mutinous, the towns-people disappointed. Priests who were sent to visit Joan in her cell to find out if the horrifying rumours of her lapse from grace were true were set upon and threatened, called 'Armagnac traitors,' and had to take to their heels.

Cauchon came on the Monday morning with a strong escort. Joan told him roundly that she had reassumed her page's suit because he had not kept his word to her that she should be taken out of irons and allowed to hear Mass, and go to some place where there would be other women about her. She admitted she had heard her Voices again, and that through them God had sent her His pity, that in her weakness and fear of the fire she had abjured Him, and damned her soul to save her body.

It was enough. Cauchon summoned his forty-one assessors and put it to the vote. It was unanimously decided, while the crowd and the

English troops outside in the streets muttered and threatened, to hand her over to the secular arm, with the request that gentleness be shown— a mere matter of form in this case, as there could be no verdict but death, and that a cruel one. In view of the fact that she had admitted doubt as to the heavenly nature of her Voices she might be considered penitent on that score and be allowed to receive the last Sacrament.

Ladvenu broke the news to her and records how pitifully she wept and cried: 'Alas, that I should be so cruelly treated, and my uncorrupted body burned to ashes this day!' She complained to him of the violence and misery she had endured as a prisoner among debased men. To Cauchon, who came to pay her a valedictory visit, she said sternly: 'Bishop, I die through you.' He cannot have been easy in his mind. He had earlier threatened [two of his assessors with punishment when they pointed out that the trial was invalid because all present were prejudiced against the prisoner.

His *pulchrum processum*, his beautiful trial that had begun so well, was not rounding off gracefully; there was an uncomfortable air of apology about these final stages, and he must have deeply resented being hustled and browbeaten by his English masters. He had declared under Warwick's sardonic eye that he was concerned only with the salvation of the Maid's soul; he now reproached her with having retracted her abjuration and pointed out that she had invited punishment. He left her to the consolation of her confessions, and went to prepare himself for his public appearance.

The Sacrament was brought into the cell, carelessly, on a dish, without any of the usual accompaniments. Ladvenu sent for candles and robes suitable to the occasion, and spoke the office for the dying over Joan's bent and shorn head.

She received the Sacrament with tears; to Pierre Maurice, whose persuasive sermon had so shaken her, she asked: 'Maître Pierre, where shall I be tonight?' Pierre Maurice answered with gentleness: 'Have you not faith in Our Lord?' to which she replied: 'Yes, and God willing I shall soon be with my Saints in Paradise.' (Not in that hateful cell, mocked at and man-handled, a prey to hideous doubts and self-torment.)

She was dressed in a long, grey penitent's robe and was conducted outside to where a cart was waiting, stumbling in her unaccustomed skirts, worn from sleeplessness and fasting, grimy and pallid, her shorn head bare, and taken with an armed escort to the old market place, where the stake was. She was shown to the judges on their dais and to the people, and then stood dumbly listening to the funeral sermon delivered by Nicolas Midi. When he had finished Cauchon rose and reminded her (speaking also for the silent Lemaistre) that after abjuration of her errors, she had 'fallen again—Oh sorrow!—into these errors and crimes as the dog returns to his vomit.' Solemnly he pronounced her abandoned by the Church, cast off, and given over to the secular arm.

In silence after he had ceased speaking, Joan knelt, and before them all prayed aloud. It was recorded afterwards that many in the crowd wept with her. Nicolas Loiselleur was overcome and left the market place; Manchon, the little clerk, hid his face, unable to bear the scene. He was well paid for his work during the trial, and afterwards bought a missal as a souvenir, which he used to pray from, for her soul's repose.

A new stake had been built on a high erection of plaster so that she had to be lifted up on to it. A dunce's cap was placed on her head, bearing two demons rampant and the hideous words: '*Heretic, relapsed, apostate, idolatress.*' Though she was a tall woman she must have looked very small, so high up there above the heads of the crowd. The executioner had difficulty in getting near her, she was so far away.

Massieu, Ladvenu, and Ysambard de la Pierre remained as close to her as they could. The two latter were devout young men, the former anything but virtuous. But he braved the flames to be near her. He had thrust into her hand, as she was dragged to the stake, a little rough cross of two bits of firewood, which an English soldier made for her.

The crowd, from being impatient, had grown frightened and silent; some of the English soldiers called to Cauchon to ask if he meant to make them dine there. He signalled the *bailli* in charge and the lowest faggots were kindled.

Joan looked all about her and was heard to sigh: 'Ah, Rouen, I have great fear you will suffer for my death.' Ysambard de la Pierre had been hurriedly dispatched to the nearest church and now came running with a tall crucifix in his hands. Ladvenu took it from him and climbed on to the piled faggots in order to bring it within her sight. She was heard to call in a clear voice on her Saints; through the ascending smoke they appeared to her in brightness as of old. An Englishman laughed; another saw a white dove fly away; another exclaimed: 'We are lost, we have burned a Saint!'

The executioner flung oil on the lowest flames, which spread, and the smoke rose, rank and dense, and, with a vile smell of sulphur, hid her from sight. Ladvenu was plucked down before his robes began to singe, as a last cry of 'Jesus' was heard high up above their heads.

When the executioner raked aside the burning brushwood to exhibit the blackened fragment hanging from the stake, half the crowd were on their knees.

Chapter Nine

The Recovery of France

TWENTY years later, the two priests, simple monks vowed to poverty and having nothing to gain and nothing to fear from the world, deposed: 'We heard her from the midst of the fire calling on her Saints and her Archangel . . . Then, as her head fell forward, she gave a great cry of "Jesus!" '[1]

Thus testified the two Dominicans, Martin Ladvenu and Ysambard de la Pierre, who had dared the choking fumes to hold the cross before her sight and to pray in her hearing. She had motioned them to climb down when the fire grew hot. Their recollection, even after many years, of that May morning was still vivid; of the laughter of the crowd turning to uneasy silence, then to mounting hysteria; of the English soldier who had sworn to throw a log on the bonfire, and who had in the same moment seen a white dove fly out of her mouth; of the anxious executioner coming to be shriven, crying out that God would never forgive him for his part in burning a Saint. It left no doubt in their minds that they had been present at a martyrdom.

[1] *Jeanne d'Arc*, Jules Michelet.

After the body, from which the clothing had been burnt away, was exposed to the general view, Cauchon and his followers hurried from the scene to avoid possible demonstrations of hostility. Orders of the strictest had been given to the executioner that no relics of the Maid were to be sold. But the heart and entrails refused to burn. The executioner threw them into the Seine, and in superstitious terror sought out the friendly Ysambard to make confession.

Outwardly Joan's life was over. Bedford could congratulate himself. The great two years of reconquest of which she had been the moving spirit had passed like a breath, and Charles was still only a King in name. Joan's successes and her fame were localized in the vicinity of the Loire; the trial and martyrdom at Rouen made little stir in an age when suspected persons were frequently tried and executed for heresy.

The English soldier who handed her the rough cross of sticks, and the faggot-thrower who saw her soul escape in the form of a dove, spent that night in a tavern, comforting and reassuring themselves; and the English clerk who called out in a panic that all was lost since they had burnt a Saint received, no doubt, a sharp reprimand from his master, Cardinal Beaufort. The heart of the Maid was safe at the bottom of the Seine, and soon only a scorched patch on the cobbles of the Old Market Place would indicate where the stake had stood. Bedford could rest assured that the legend had been destroyed, along with all that had once been mortal of Joan of Dom-rémy. The proceedings of her long, just, and careful trial would be placed on record for all the world to see.

But legends are not so easily disposed of. They go underground, as water does, only to gush out in unexpected places and at odd times. After her death she was seen in many different places; praying alone in the fields, mingling with the faithful at Mass, riding at nightfall with a ghostly company of soldiers, the smoke of the burning hanging about her as if she had come from tending an autumn bonfire.

The examination of witnesses for her rehabili-tation in 1450, though well-meaning, produced a mass of confused and unreliable testimony. It had, like the proceedings at Rouen, a political bias. Jean Beaupère, an extremely clever man, admitted at the Rehabilitation that there was more of human intention and natural causes than of the supernatural in her story; he had never believed her to be a witch. But he attributed to her a share of feminine guile and subtlety which it is certain she did not possess. Her second assessors were anxious to prove that since she had received direct revelation from God she was outside the laws made by man. They had to take a stand on the corruptness of her judges, and in doing so made her an innocent victim of political animosity.

Posterity accepted the saccharine convention, and made insipid statues of her, decently petti-coated; plaster images that bore no resemblance to the real Joan, the warm-hearted, contradictory creature who exasperated the learned men of her day, cajoled a reluctant King, and gathered the sorrows of France to her warm heart, that heart that the flames were powerless to consume.

The friends of her childhood and youth, after their dull recollection had been stimulated, produced a confused impression which tends to blur the clear picture formed without difficulty from her own words and actions. It was too easy to sentimentalize her; at the trial for the Rehabilitation the men who had voted to put her to the torture assisted most eagerly in the good work. But the men who knew what she had been really like—the common soldiers who had fought with her at Orléans, at Jargeau, at Compiègne—could not convey it.

The attempt of M. Anatole France in our own time to make of her a stick with which to castigate the Church, and the kindly efforts of Mr. Andrew Lang to rescue her from M. France's irreverence, neither detract from nor add to her stature. Joan, the broad-shouldered peasant with her roughly-shorn cap of black hair, her deep voice, and her compelling personality, suffers equally at the hands of iconoclasts and sentimentalists.

The question arises, What would have

happened to her if the Church had, after all, been unable to convict her, or if her friends had rallied and snatched her from prison? What if Charles had displayed a belated gratitude and raised a ransom for her, or the Archbishop excommunicated Cauchon and discredited the findings of the Bishop's Court?

It is impossible to imagine. One is inclined to believe that she had to die because, as the world was not ready for her, her sphere of usefulness was limited. When she perished on that May morning for her stubborn, foolhardy, invincible contentions, her short life of nineteen years and four months was complete. It was a masterpiece. Never in all the long history of mankind has one human being stood up alone before the allied might of Church and State, and with such good humour, patience, courage, and stubborn faith as Joan showed, conducted a solitary defence. I do not personally believe in her abjuration. I believe she was worn out with imprisonment under peculiarly barbaric and horrible circumstances. She had been questioned and exhorted day and night till her head swam, and, from recent illness, lack of exercise, and prolonged fasting, was probably light-headed. The form of the abjuration published after her death was lengthy; witnesses of the actual scene said that the form Erard produced for her to sign was brief as a Paternoster. Most probably she was only required to confess to having broken the

Divine Law and the canon laws, 'by wearing a dissolute, ill-shaped, and immodest dress against the decency of nature,' and to promise in future 'to dwell in the unity of Our Holy Mother the Church and in the obedience of Our Holy Father, the Pope of Rome.' She signed in the belief that abjuration would deliver her from the secular arm and place her in an ecclesiastical prison among women. She did not ever intend to renounce the source of her inspiration, her beloved Voices.

And this brings us to the question which each must resolve according to personal conviction. Were her Voices the product of her own imagination?

It was a richly imaginative age. The Saints were ever-present in people's minds, kindly, attentive intercessors, half-human, half-divine. The Church might keep its dogmatic theology, but that would not suit a people who were 'indifferent to metaphysics and prompted by a longing to feel the objects of its worship in close proximity and to love them.' To appease this longing they selected the tender and human legends of the Saints, and made them an indissoluble part of their everyday lives, and men accorded to the Virgin the courtly gallantry shown by a Knight to his lady, as a superior but still feminine being.

The Virgin would have been less human to a child like Joan, who loved action and thrilled to traveller's tales of high, heroic deeds, than St. Michael the Archangel, thrusting down Satan beneath his flying feet. Saint Margaret was the poor peasant-woman's Saint, a gentle creature who had died at Antioch in defence of her virginity. Saint Catherine, the royal Egyptian, was of sterner mettle, and had been adopted as a patron Saint by the University of Paris, for having argued successfully against the pagan scholars who tried to tempt her to renounce her faith in favour of false gods; she had been martyred by the order of the Roman Emperor Maximian, and carried to Heaven in the arms of angels. She was the patron of virgins, as well as theologians.

Joan was familiar with the crude representations of these two in the churches of Domrémy and Maxey, and since it was the habit of her contemporaries to single out a particular Saint or Saints, and honour them with small courtesies, she had fixed her childish affections on these two, the pure Margaret, the royal and militant Catherine.

It was plausibly suggested at her trial that Joan's heavenly visitors had appeared to her in the guise in which she was accustomed to picture them, and that their voices were audible to her only when the church bells up and down the valley were ringing.

Bells have a strong, emotional appeal, as Shakespeare knew when he wrote:

'If ever you have looked on better days;
If ever been where bells have knolled to
    Church;
If ever sat at any good man's feast;
If ever from your eyelids wiped a tear
And knew what 'tis to pity and be pitied. . . .'

It is true, her companions confirmed it, that
Joan, during the ringing of the bells, and in the
deep hush that followed after they had ceased to
ring, was moved to tears and prayer; in those
moments she was very close to her Saints.
Heaven to her childish mind lay all about her.
It was only a short step from the imagination to
the reality; but was the reality any the less real
for that? She was not a neglected or an ill-used
child, who might, for solace or to attract notice,
invent imaginary companions. According to
several of her childhood's friends, she blushed
when told she was too devout and went to Church
too often. This was surely not exhibitionism.

A nineteenth-century historian has said drily
but justly: 'We cannot pretend to explain the
surprising story of the Maid of Orléans; for,
however easy it may be to suppose that a heated
and enthusiastic imagination produced her visions,
it is a much greater problem to account for the
credit they obtained, and for the success that
attended her.'[1]

The appearance of her Saints she could never

[1] Hallam: *Europe During the Middle Ages.*

be got to describe, beyond vague allusions to clouds of light and rare and precious crowns. She saw and avoided the trap the prosecution set for her, and denied with scorn that she had held revel in the Fairy Wood, or carried a mandrake in her bosom, or had communication with spirits other than holy.

After she had left her father's roof for ever, the Voices went with her, and it seems she could summon them at need. It is difficult not to feel that she sometimes embroidered their communications, and one finds oneself in occasional sympathy with Charles and his advisers when they were expected to receive and meekly obey the Voices' mandates, delivered in Joan's most dictatorial tones.

During her imprisonment her Saints visited her hourly, and even spoke in her ear in presence of the assembled judges. At the end it was testified on her behalf by the two monks who were closest to her, that her Saints appeared to her in brightness, loving, welcoming, forgiving; and few of us, I think, would doubt that it was so.

However we try to pin her down and explain her, Joan eludes us and goes her own way. The secular arm that set the faggots alight under her, had it been able to put its judgment into colloquial English, would have summed her up as a damned nuisance. She had thrust herself, this peasant from the valley of the Meuse, into the councils of princes, into the light that beat upon the very throne of France. She was not humble save in the presence of her God; she could be haughty with her betters, downright with her fellow captains, unrelentingly obstinate, uncompromisingly truthful. At the trial for her Rehabilitation these were conveniently forgotten and emphasis was laid on her maiden piety; in seeking to make her out a Saint they made a fool of her.

Uncompromising as she could be in matters relating to her sacred mission, she was not without lovable human foibles. She loved rich accoutrements and royal pageantry. It was a delight to her to ride a horse of mettle, she who had never aspired beyond a jog on a cart horse at harvest time. She was indifferent to the homeliness of her features, but wrapped herself in a red velvet cloak such as a prince might have worn, loving the bright colour and the soft texture. She could rally the armies of France, and next moment weep for a dying enemy.

She was equal to all the varying demands made on her. 'She solved the problem; she assumed the manners; she faced the rain of arrows and bullets; she faced the Doctors and Clerks; she animated the soldiery in Napoleon's way; she spoke and acted like a captain, like a clerk, like a *grande dame de par le monde*, as the need of the moment required.' So Andrew Lang explains her, and though there is a touch of generous over-statement in the tribute, it contains the plain truth about Joan. Without education, without any experience of the world, she took on a great mission and carried it to a foretold conclusion, succeeding where the worldly, the greedy, the plausible, and the defeatists had failed.

As an historian of her times[1] has pointed out, the English hated Joan with purely political hatred, the Church with an abstract theological hatred, the French gentry with a much more personal hatred because she was successful, pious, and of peasant derivation. Only the French people had loved her, and they were still of no account.

The soul of her beloved France was struggling out of the deep mud into which a fiercely individualistic oligarchy had thrust it. Joan embodied in herself the sturdy self-reliance and the shrewd realism that were to become characteristics of a great nation. She lived her short life intensely and met a terrible death in order that her country's soul might grow. Her vision endures; her unquenchable gaiety and her obstinate courage have passed into the soil of France and into the blood of Frenchmen.

By October 1431, Bedford was ready to begin preparations for his nephew's coronation, which took place on the 16th of December. It was a

[1] Sir J. H. Ramsay.

hole-and-corner affair, conducted hurriedly for fear of interference from partisans of the French King or the Maid, who might be roaming the country in search of a fight. Poton de Saintrailles had been captured in an attempt to enter Rouen three months earlier. (If Joan had still been a prisoner there she would have heard what she had vainly listened for day after day, the ringing battle-cry of: '*For God and the Maid*', and the familiar uproar of an *escarmouche*.)

The Cardinal of England, great-uncle of the ten-year-old King, placed on his head the crown of France. The Bishops of Paris and Thérouanne sat by and took no part, and the ceremony was conducted according to English rather than French precedent. The canopy that covered the boy King in his progress from the Regent's residence to Notre Dame was carried by representatives of the Guilds of the City of Paris. Otherwise the congregation was composed of Englishmen, lean and wary men who remembered Henry V's great days; Bedford, who had sworn to preserve his dead brother's empire; Warwick, who had watched the Maid burn; Suffolk and Salisbury and York.

According to a contemporary the coronation banquet was a wretched affair, and so badly organized that high academic dignitaries had to go without seats, while mere onlookers, who had only come to stare and get a free meal, seized the best places. Henry VI had not inaugurated his reign with lavishness; he allowed the University of Paris tax exemption in return for its support at the Trial of the Maid (he could hardly do less) but released no prisoners, as was the custom, and distributed no largesse to the poor. His stay in his new capital was extremely brief; he had time to exchange a visit of courtesy with the elderly, painted wreck who had once been the notorious Queen Isabelle, and who was his maternal grandmother, and left, in ungracious silence on the part of the Parisians, who felt defrauded. 'A bourgeois marrying off one of his daughters would have done the thing better,' was the general verdict. Bedford had neither the funds nor the inclination to be lavish; the Trial of the Maid had already cost the English Treasury a pretty penny.

In the English King's triumphal procession was a half-witted shepherd boy whom the English had captured, who purported to have miraculous visions. The Archbishop of Rheims had produced him to soothe the people's fears and to take Joan's place; being witless, he was far more biddable and in greater awe of his superiors than the Maid. The English were able to make much shorter work of him; after the coronation he was sewn up in a sack and thrown into the Seine.

The Church was so far justified in its condemnation of Joan; her inspiration, however genuine in itself, set an example for a number of charlatans, all purporting to be divinely inspired. A woman, called Catherine de la Rochelle, had tried to enlist the Maid's powerful support for her own visions, and on being proved a fraud by Joan, who had a breezy way with other people's inspirations, had given malicious evidence against her which was used at the trial without regard to the unreliable character of the witness.

That winter the Seine was frozen over. It was the coldest winter in the recollection of any living, and the plight of the people of Paris was piteous. The English and Burgundians had drained the city and blocked its supply routes. It seemed as if the Parisians were equally poorly off, whoever they called master—little Henry the Plantagenet, or knock-kneed Charles the Valois. Burgundy, who had been the people's hero, was not so high in favour, for had he not sold them to the stern Regent Duke?—a cold man who permitted no pageantry, though he reformed the prisons and tried to control the Black Market, where goods changed hands at fabulous prices while the poor went empty.

'For the poor of Paris, who in those years lived mainly on turnip tops and miscellaneous refuse, life must have been a grinding torment.' The cold was so intense that empty houses were torn down and broken up for fuel. Many died; only the hardiest survived in hope of better times when peace should come again. It was slow in coming, but it was on the way. Since

Henry V's death as the English hold on France slowly weakened, the interrelation of the two countries, outcome of consanguinity and proximity, also waned. English blossomed with Chaucer as the language of poetry, and by the first quarter of the fifteenth century the use of it had superseded French in legal documents and for the purposes of government. It was too early still for the Renaissance, on its way from the South and East, to attempt to revive their unity with the language of classical antiquity. 'As England and France went further forward on the road of national self-expression, there arose an increasing contrast of temperaments.' As far back as the start of the Hundred Years War the growing spirit of English nationalism had bred the belief in Englishmen that England was the cradle of a superior race. The tendency of the Englishman to hide this conviction by assuming indifference or self-depreciation did not endear him to his more logical and idealistic neighbour. 'Henceforth each country was destined to live a life of its own, a more national, but a more restricted life.'

The immediate cause of the weakening of the English stranglehold on France was partly the political situation in England, which more and more took toll of Bedford's energies. By the end of 1431 tentative peace had been agreed to between Burgundy and the French King, a truce of six years' duration which withdrew the Burgundian armies from the field, though bands of Burgundian freebooters continued to range northern France, fighting for the side that paid them best.

Joan's old friend, de Boussac, made an abortive attempt to retake Rouen. The Bastard of Orléans seized Chartres by a trick; soldiers were smuggled into the town hidden under sacks of salt. Bedford made a strong bid to recover Lagny, but the Bastard and Raoul de Gaucourt frustrated him with Joan's own technique of a pretence attack on one gate while reinforcements were being poured in at another.

That year (1432) the Duchess of Bedford died, Burgundy's gentle sister, who had sent Joan a dress in prison and had tried to intervene to prevent her being man-handled by the English guards. She was mourned as having been the good and the well-loved friend of the people of Paris.

Meanwhile, Charles at Chinon was a prey to inertia. There had been a great deal of shouting, and a lot, as he considered, of misdirected energy on the part of the Maid, which had gained him exactly nothing but a hollow title, which he couldn't use. The seesaw of war went on, the French retook towns from the English, and the Burgundians seized them back again; it had been happening for a very long time. All the autumn and winter of 1433, news kept coming in of the retaking by Burgundy of a number of towns in Champagne—thus nullifying the non-aggression pact made two years earlier. To their credit be it said that the men who had fought with Joan were not ready to accept so tamely the reversal of her achievements. The Constable de Richemont, disgusted at the disgraceful apathy of his King and the insolent ascendancy of La Trémoille, entered into a conspiracy with the element at Court that was not defeatist or self-seeking, led by the Queen's brother, Charles of Anjou, son of the forcible Yolande of Sicily.

La Trémoille, that mountain of a man, was surprised at night in his bed in the Tour de Coudray, where Joan had lodged four years earlier. News was brought to the terrified King that the man who had dominated him and the fortunes of France for so long was overthrown; it was announced that he had been murdered by a dagger-thrust in the stomach, but a counter rumour said that he had paid out a fortune in ransom from his ill-gotten store. Whatever the truth, he had toppled from his eminence. The King, in a panic, for he greatly feared his surly Constable, turned to his brother-in-law for reassurance, and the House of Anjou once more began to ascend.

With such energetic counsellors as Charles of Anjou and his brother Réné, Dunois, and de Richemont, Charles was to show a belated enthusiasm for war; in later years, influenced by his mistress, Agnes Sorel, on behalf of the common people from whom she derived, he was to achieve a lukewarm popularity.

242

Bedford was well aware of the rifts impending. It had always been his ungrateful task to conciliate Burgundy. After the death of his Duchess— too soon after—he had married again a niece of the Bishop of Thérouanne, Jacqueline of Luxembourg. Philip of Burgundy expressed himself as hurt and offended, both at the slight to his sister's memory, and at the presumption of the House of Luxembourg. After that there was coldness and estrangement between the two old allies. Bedford's position was perpetually threatened by the mischief-making propensities of his younger brother, Humfry of Gloucester. So greatly was his steadying influence missed in England that Parliament, on his next visit, put a petition before him to remain and accept the Regency for the Crown.

But his heart was in France. He told the young King in Council: 'I have found the multitude of your subjects there as well-disposed and as desirous to keep their faith and truth to your Highness as ever were people, and to me as loving and as kind.' The thought of capitulation was evidently in his mind when he added how great a pity it would be to lose that noble realm 'for the getting and keeping of which my lord that was your father, to whose soul God do mercy, and many other noble princes . . . have paid their lives.'

There was no more money forthcoming to finance the war; that was the dismal truth. So

lean was the English Treasury at that time that
Cardinal Beaufort had to make a private loan
to provide the Regent of France, on his return
journey, with a necessary escort.

Bedford found Normandy in a state of revolt
from the activities of *écorcheurs*, professional
soldiers of all parties, so called because they
flayed their victims of all they possessed to their
very shirts. Some of Joan's partisans led
these free-lance adventurers, who provoked the
peasants until they retaliated and were brutally
suppressed. A change of front on the part of
Burgundy did not make his burden lighter. The
political aspect was changing; now that the
French King had for Ministers of the Crown
men of honour and enterprise, the monarchy
was no longer a sham. The Duke of Bourbon,
who had fought with Joan when he was Count
of Clermont, and the Constable de Richemont
had both married sisters of Philip of Burgundy.
A meeting between the three brothers-in-law
was arranged and an elaborate reconciliation
staged with much pageantry. Philip, with the
utmost affability, declared his cousinly affection
for King Charles. No mention was made of the
murder of Duke John the Fearless at the bridge
of Montéreau, but it was tacitly recognized
that the time had come to allow the ancient
quarrel to lapse.

England had for so long been obliged to
truckle to Burgundy, that the Duke thought it

would be the easiest thing in the world to bring the English to heel. His optimism was hardly justified. The Congress of Arras was called for August 1435, and terms for peace were laid before the English delegates. The French terms were not ungenerous; the King of England was to give up unconditionally the title of King of France, and the right to add the French lilies to the leopards of England. But in compensation he was to retain the Kingdom of Guienne and almost all of Normandy. The English were unbending; the most they would consent to was a lengthy truce, and for no consideration at all would King Henry renounce the right his father had won to the crown of France. In years to come English statesmen were to regret bitterly this refusal. Bedford's influence was absent from the Congress; Cardinal Beaufort, who took his place, was an imperialist of an earlier epoch.

It was the pretext which Burgundy, the opportunist, had been looking for. When the last effort of the French—a proposal to shelve the whole question of the renunciation till King Henry should come of age, the English in the meanwhile to evacuate certain agreed-on areas— was repudiated, he announced his obligations to his old ally to be at an end. The Church sanctioned it. The power of Burgundy was so inflated that Charles' advisers thought it prudent, no doubt with certain mental reservations, to accept Duke Philip's friendship on his own terms, which included the ceding of almost the whole of Picardy, so that eastern France was now entirely under his hand.

Bedford's life's work was over. It was now September. On the 15th of the month at his house in Rouen, between one and two in the morning, the great Englishman died in his bed, worn out by the complexities of his inherited task. He had brought to it a disenchanted sense of obligation. 'Firm, just and conciliatory, he governed France in the spirit of the men who have built up England's colonial empire.'[1]

'Noble in birth and worth; wise, liberal, feared and loved,' was to be the tribute of the French. He was buried in Rouen, not far from the spot where Joan had died.

The word 'peace' was on everyone's lips. Philip of Burgundy, with characteristic choice of a dramatic moment, chose the anniversary of his father's murder to announce his intention of seeking reconciliation with the French King. Eleven days later the long, bitter quarrel was brought formally to an end, and the Burgundian and Armagnac factions were declared reconciled.

Inflamed by Humfry of Gloucester, who was quite without the political *flair* of his brothers, England turned angrily against her own interests, and denounced false Philip. It was a foolish act, which Bedford would never have permitted, and led to a breach with Flanders which seriously

[1] Sir J. H. Ramsay.

affected the trade conditions of both countries. But the English and Burgundians had been companions-in-arms for fifteen years; the old alliance was not to be dissolved in a moment. Burgundian soldiers joined in an English attack on the French garrison of St. Denis, where Joan had laid her armour before the high altar of the Cathedral. It fell in October, the last notable victory the English were to enjoy. One by one the towns of northern France expelled the English occupation and declared themselves subject to the Valois.

The Captain of Paris was Lord Willoughby, whom the French called 'de Wilbi.' He was assisted in his unenviable task by the Burgundian Bishop of Thérouanne, whose sympathies were not so much pro-English as anti-French. In the spring of 1436 many adjacent towns had fallen to the reorganized armies of France under the new Marshal, l'Isle-Adam. In April, all Paris citizens were required to retake the Oath of Allegiance to the King of England; the articles of the Treaty of Troyes were hollowly reaffirmed by the University, the Law, the Exchequer, the City Guilds and other public bodies. If there was a grumbling undertone of dissension from the people, it was attributed to the poor conditions of living in Paris at that time, owing to the English depredations on the surrounding country. Willoughby perhaps could not afford to take too much notice; his situation was extremely precarious, since the garrison under him was too small to defend the city effectively in case of attack.

De Richemont and l'Isle-Adam waited; while letters, seemingly innocent, passed in and out of Paris, so that that grey early morning of April 13th, 1436, found those forewarned wakeful in their beds, straining to hear the sound of an army's approach.

The Seine ran under the city in those days, and its many bridges were crowded with double rows of tall, crooked houses, their gabled upper storeys jutting out over the water. On the left bank lay the warren that was the University of Paris. During the English rule the streets were closed at night by chains. At each of the gates of the city with their twin towers, a guard walked the broad parapet along the wall, and watched the approaches from Beauvais on the north, Meaux on the east, Mantes on the west, Melun on the south.

Just before sunrise, when the sky was brightening, de Richemont approached the city at the Porte St. Michel, and sent one of his officers forward, carrying the King's Standard. The St. Michael's gate was barred, but the sentry pointed silently eastward toward the Porte St. Jacques. There, without hindrance, the drawbridge was unloosed and the invaders (Dunois among them) entered the sleeping city. The Marshal l'Isle-Adam climbed to the top of the Tour St. Jacques and hoisted the white standard with the gold lilies. Orderly and unhurried, the soldiers marched in without opposition. A proclamation of an amnesty for Parisians was hung up in the market place. De Richemont, with his captains, rode soberly to Notre Dame. The priests were celebrating early Mass when the party of armed men clanked into the Cathedral and knelt among the sparse worshippers. Joan would have rejoiced in the scene, but Joan would not have been able to emulate the Constable's undramatic manner in a situation so full of dramatic possibilities.

Willoughby, taken wholly by surprise, roused his garrison and called on his supporters. But the people took charge. They had trembled and fled to their holes when it was rumoured that the Maid was at their gates; Bedford's astute propaganda had made them dread Armagnac's reprisals. But the famine of the last two winters had changed their fears to anger and desperation. They turned on the English garrison with stolen arms and stones, and put up the chains across the streets to hinder them. The uproar grew, as the Bishops tried to make themselves heard, but were shouted down. There was no choice for Willoughby but to call off his followers and retire into the fortress of the Bastille. The University withdrew sullenly within its walls.

De Richemont proclaimed, on the King's behalf, a general pardon; he presented Willoughby with fair terms, which were found acceptable, and the English garrison, under escort, marched out of Paris on April the 17th, without any display or demonstration. They were allowed to go without rancour; some rude spirits in the crowd yelled after them '*Au renard! a la queue!*'— an allusion to the fox's brush which Henry V had adopted as his cognizance, or perhaps to the generally-held belief of the French that Englishmen had tails. Willoughby, as a prisoner of war, was sent to Rouen; the Bishop of Thérouanne, who had once sold the Maid's armour at a profit, was returned to his diocese. Thus, with scarcely any blood-letting, the rule of the English in Paris was over.

The English rule in France was waning '... it was no longer a question whether England could maintain her footing in France.' (Without Burgundy to wage war for her, England had not the means to prosecute it.) 'Only the pace of her reluctant withdrawal remained to be settled.'[1] Reluctant it was, and correspondingly slow. After all, the war had been going on for ninety-odd years—the longest-lived had been babes-in-arms when Edward III struck at Crécy. The men who had been young and vigorous when the Treaty of Troyes was made, were far into middle age. The existing state of affairs had been so long established that both peoples had grown apathetic, the English to a

[1] H. A. L. Fisher.

perpetual financial problem, the French to the depredations of mercenary soldiers. Just as many of the Conqueror's followers had settled down in England, so many Englishmen and Scots found a congenial way of life in France, attaching themselves to whichever local faction paid them best, without regard to politics. When finally, in the early autumn of 1449, Rouen capitulated, many of the English soldiers pleaded that as they had married French women, and as their children were wholly French, they might be allowed to remain as subjects of the French King. Rouen had been in English hands for thirty years.

England was beginning to be enfeebled by the internal quarrels that were eventually to plunge it into civil war. France was tending toward the establishment of an absolute monarchy. Charles, whose energy and initiative were beginning to wake, put down a threatened revolt in 1440 with some skill. His nearest of kin, remembering their ancient feudal privileges, and unable to believe that they had not still got a puppet King to overbear, banded themselves together with the young Dauphin Louis at their head. (Contempt for the King was so generally felt, and no doubt shown, that it had even divided his family.) The faction that numbered d'Alençon, the Bastard of Orléans, Charles, Duke of Bourbon, and the Counts of Vendôme and Armagnac—all royal, all closely knit by heredity and ties of old

251

association to the House of Valois—took violent exception to an ordinance for the suppression of private levies, and the imposition of a permanent tax to provide a standing army for the Crown. This innovation, known as the Grande Ordonnance, menaced their personal prestige, and struck at the roots of feudal privilege. Yet it has persisted to this day; the foundation of France's standing army. By inaugurating fixed pay for the soldiers, it removed the incitement to brigandage. It also deprived the feudal nobility of a strong weapon of aggression. By being unexpectedly both conciliatory and firm, Charles bought off his critics, and deflected their energies to the retaking of Normandy. He himself fought in person, and with some distinction, at the final relief of Pontoise in 1441, but sullied the triumph by ordering three hundred English prisoners to be flung naked and trussed into the Seine.

During the next eight years Charles maintained this perilous ascendancy, backed by a section of the rich bourgeoisie. In England there was much unrest and misrule. Henry VI was quite unable to rise to the demands made on him. He was loved forgivingly by the common people, who recognized in the saintly, ineffectual creature another Edward the Confessor. 'But he had not manhood enough to rule a convent, much less to rule feudal England. His slender faculties broke down under the strain of over-training and premature responsibility.' He was more interested in trying to obtain consent for the canonization of King Alfred than in the pressing question of how or where to raise more money to prosecute the war with France.

In the cause of international peace Henry agreed to the necessity for a French marriage. The choice fell on Margaret, daughter of *le bon roi* Réné of Anjou, titular King of Sicily, in effect a penniless prince, who was ready to ask a good price for his daughter. To purchase the alliance King Henry was induced, through his ambassador Suffolk, to cede the English possessions in Maine to the lady's father. The price was too much. The English were sick of foreigners (Henry V's widow had been a French princess with a taste for remarriage) and it was bitter to part with so valuable and integral a part of their heritage as the province of Maine, for the sake of another dowerless princess. The Earl of Suffolk, who had commanded the armies of England against those of France, led by the Maid of Orléans (*Chuffort* was what Joan called him, she could never get her tongue round these slippery English names), was a connection of the Beauforts, who had virtually controlled English internal affairs since Henry V, on his deathbed, gave the Regency into their hands. The name of Suffolk became associated with the loss of Maine, since he had transacted the business side of the French marriage. With the Beauforts behind him, the young Queen at his side pressing for peace with France, the Earl enjoyed a period of political despotism, his old rival, Humfry of Gloucester, being now dead. He, no doubt, honestly believed that by surrendering a part, England could concentrate better on retaining her more vital interests in Normandy and Guienne. 'This fatal concession, wrung from an unwary diplomatist in a moment of weakness, became at once the turning-point of English politics'—or at all events the turning-point in the fortunes of the House of Lancaster. Maine was not allowed to lapse without a delaying action on the part of England which weakened the English garrisons and gave France's military leaders time to repair and reorganize. Eventually, Henry was obliged to send his old friend and ally into banishment, hoping to save him from the vengeance of his political opponents, but the Earl was followed, taken at sea, and put to death.

Violence, disgrace, and tragedy dogged the protagonists in the drama of the Maid. Only King Charles, who deserted her, escaped retribution. But he was a broken-hearted man when Agnes Sorel died, and lonely when his son turned against him.

Joan had said confidently that the English would lose a greater stake than Orléans; that they would eventually lose all they held in France. By 1450 the last town in Normandy had flung out its English masters. The retaking of Rouen rounds off the heroic story of Joan. One feels it

fitting that it was Dunois, as the King's Lieu-
tenant-General, who watched the garrison ride
out.

In the same year, Brittany was freed of such
English troops as adhered to their posts; Château
Gaillard fell, and the port of Harfleur, where
Henry V's first expeditionary force had landed.
Everywhere, in Gascony, in the Cotentin and the
Vexin, towns rolled over like ninepins before the
armies of France.

By 1452 Guienne and Gascony were retaken.
Having mutual trade interests, their attitude to
the English occupation was not coloured by
hostility; being a more warm-hearted people,
they saw their English allies of ancient standing
routed out with some regrets.

The prospect of the loss of Bordeaux, hallowed
in Englishmen's imagination by its association
with the Black Prince, sent a deep shudder of
alarm through England. As a last, desperate
measure the elderly Earl of Shrewsbury, the
dreaded Talbot of the siege of Orléans, was sent
with an army to its relief.

The staunch town of Castillon on the right
bank of the Dordogne was besieged by a French
force and appealed for help. The French were
attacking it with guns or culverins, an innovation
which was to mark a change in the whole technique of war. The range of one of these was
greater than that of an arrow, though it may be
questioned if it was in effect as deadly. It was

high summer and the air was full of the blinding white dust of the south; because of this, Talbot's men, underestimating the strength of the enemy, ventured too near and found themselves surrounded. The old man fell from his pony and was trodden down under a surge of attackers, and with him died the last chance of an English recovery. Bordeaux capitulated on October 19th. The Hundred Years War, that had in fact lasted sixteen years beyond the century, was at an end.

For two years clerks and doctors of theology had been working busily to collect evidence and examine witnesses as to the unassailable purity and Divine inspiration of the Maid.

In the same year that Bordeaux fell, and with it the English empire in France, the enquiry was reopened by the Grand Inquisitor of France, and Cardinal d'Estouteville, Bishop of Digne. Joan's widowed mother, Isabelle d'Arc, after nearly twenty years, appealed to the Pope to reinstate her daughter's good name. The old woman, twisted and bowed with a lifetime of hard work and ill-health, so strongly worded her appeal, so relentlessly assailed the ears of authority, that the Pope decreed the proceedings of the original trial invalid and commanded a retrial on the available evidence. He was not, of course, entirely influenced by an obscure old peasant woman from the Meuse valley. King Charles, about the same time, was coming to the same conclusion. His own efforts had proved him a true Valois, he had risen above the limitations of his nature, and perhaps recognized that he owed the Maid some credit for that regeneration. At all events, he decided that for the honour of France and its King, Joan must be placed in a suitable niche. And the only way to do that would be to denounce her original judges, and declare them full of corruption, fraud, and malice.

It was duly done, the trial for the Rehabilitation of Joan the Maid lasted over six years, till, in 1456, Calixtus III formally revoked the sentence that had been passed on her. The Church as a collective body could not err, but its members were gravely reminded that individually they were not immune from error; Cauchon's corpse was dug up and thrown into a drain.

From all over France witnesses came to Paris to testify; the mass of evidence was overwhelming. The humble people of Domrémy, her childhood associates, grown middle-aged, remembered that the daughter of Jacques d'Arc had been a good child, simple and pious. Durand Lassois was made to rack his rusty brain for corroboration. Her earliest friends, John of Metz and Bertrand de Poulengy, came out of retirement, grizzled, preoccupied, middle-aged men, soldiers of fortune turned farmers. So did Jean d'Aulon, ready to be endlessly loquacious.

Pasquerel, her confessor, told of how religion was the consuming passion of her life. Louis de Contes, who had been her little page, and had preserved something of his boyish hero-worship of her, d'Alençon, no longer young, Dunois, grave, kind and reliable as ever, gave their testimonies. So did a Carmelite Friar who had been one of the Council of Poitiers, and had been teased by Joan for his provincial way of speaking. They all solemnly testified to her virtue and sincerity, and to her military ability (which was three parts luck and one part straight common sense).

The little clerks who had taken down the report of the Trial spoke feelingly of the courage and audacity of her bearing at the time. Her answers were so wise and simple it was difficult to feel she was not inspired. There was a mass of evidence to discredit her judges, and some to prove that many among them had doubts and desired to be excused from giving judgment. Erard's servant in particular gave evidence of his master's terrible state of mind on the night before he was called upon to preach the sermon that condemned her.

At the end of it all they produced a handsome testimonial to Joan's undoubted inspiration. Almost five hundred years later it was agreed to canonize her as a Saint. She became first Joan the Venerable, then before a concourse of bishops in Rome received the decree of beatification. Another war was to sweep France, to lay waste Picardy and what had once been Philip of Burgundy's eastern principality, before it was ratified by the Pope. As St. Joan she is the Heavenly prototype of all men and women who follow their own bright star, who believe in the integrity of the soul, and who refuse to recognize failure or accept defeat.

In our end is our beginning. The Hundred Years War and the counter claims of Valois, Plantagenet, and Burgundian princes were ephemeral. They contributed nothing to the evolution of France, except inasmuch as they helped to establish the monarchy and promoted a spirit of nationalism.

The peasant, whom we saw held in the grip of feudal despotism, was beginning to make himself felt and even respected, by the end of the century. The annals of France at this time have a gaudy top-dressing of intrigue and violence, but the country's true history was being evolved in hovels and narrow streets, among peasants, poorest of the poor, and tradesmen just beginning to get rich and to control the sources of wealth— among shepherds and ploughmen, itinerant pedlars, mendicant friars, pickpockets, and inn-keepers.

Established institutions were in disrepute. The Church had made arid consistency a substitute for spiritual growth; scholarly hair-splitting on the subjects of logic and philosophy broadened no horizons, rather it reduced them. The Papacy, which should have been a rock, was divided. Love had become a courtly convention, chivalry was no longer a profession. The Feudal System, which laid a definite responsibility toward his weak dependants on the shoulders of the landowner, had lost all its original character. It was its disputatious oligarchy who brought France to the verge of dissolution; it was the sturdy, recuperative power of the peasant to rise above oppression and want which reclaimed it— the soil in fact, typified in the person of Joan of Domrémy.

Change was at hand: the Renaissance was coming from the south and east. Art was to turn back for inspiration to the simplicity of the ancient world; the study of Greek was to restore belief in the divine supremacy of reason; 'the long troubling dawn of quite a new day'[1] was breaking.

[1] Belloc.

Bibliography

SOURCES FOR THE STUDY OF THE
LIFE AND TIMES OF JOAN OF ARC

For a general survey of the period and the historical background:

A History of Europe. H. A. L. Fisher.

A History of the French People. Charles Seignobos.

Lancaster and York. Sir J. H. Ramsay (1892).

France and England in the Middle Ages and Now. T. F. Tout (Manchester University Press).

The Reign of Henry V. J. H. Wylie and W. T. Waugh.

A History of the Art of War in the Middle Ages. Sir Charles Oman.

The Mediæval Village. G. G. Coulton.

La France et l'Angleterre en Conflit. Calmette et Déprez. (Histoire générale du Moyen Age. Glotz.)

Histoire de France. Ed. Ernest Lavisse. Vol. iv. par Ch. Petit-Dutaillis.

Chronique d'Enguerrand de Monstrelet (1861). (Interesting but unreliable contemporary chronicle, edited 1836.)

LIVES OF JOAN OF ARC.

Vie de Jeanne d'Arc. Anatole France.

The Maid of France. Andrew Lang.

St. Joan of Arc. V. Sackville-West.

Jeanne d'Arc. Jules Michelet.

Aperçus nouveaux sur Jeanne d'Arc. Jules Quicherat (1856).

THE TRIAL.

Procès du Condamnation et de Réhabilitation de Jeanne d'Arc. Jules Quicherat (Paris, 1861). (Source of almost all we know about Joan: re-edited in 1921 by Champion.)

The Trial of Jeanne d'Arc. Translated from the original by W. P. Barrett.

Jeanne d'Arc, Maid of Orleans. T. Douglas Murray (another translation).

261

Index

262

INDEX

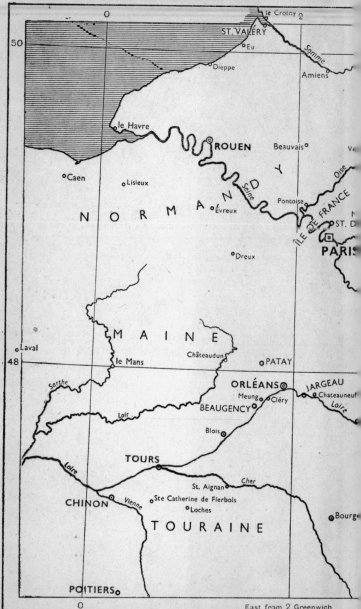